Don't Stop The World

CLARKE MACDONALD

The United Church of Canada
Toronto

Publisher: R.L. Naylor
Editor: Frank Barrett

Cover Design and Illustration: Marianne MacClellan

Dedication:

To those without whose love, support and tolerance, the kind of ministry I have tried to exercise over the years would have been quite impossible:

Muriel — "The woman beside me", for over forty years; and our children Paul, Brian and Rose Marie, with gratitude and affection.

Table of Contents

	Page
Dedication	i
Introduction	iii
Foreword by Hugh McCullum	vii
Don't Stop the World	1
A Faith for Tough Times	15
Both Sides Now	27
The Christ Mind in Ministry	39
The Church Under the Cross	51
Amazing Grace	61
The Church and Politics	71
Telling My Story — Sharing My Faith	83
Prophets Then and Prophets Now	95
Planet at the Crossroads	105
The Voice of the Unknown Soldier	115
Prayer — A Personal Approach	125
Postlude: Faith — Love and Prayer — These Three	135
Suggestions for Reflection and Discussion	142

INTRODUCTION

There can be only one valid reason for publishing a book of sermons and addresses. It must be because one believes that sharing in writing the words which have been spoken will be helpful to someone else and be a witness to the Good News. It would be felicitious, but true to say that a number of people have requested this to be done. Anyway, here as the traditional marriage service says: "for better or for worse", is the result of acting upon that suggestion.

I have been very much helped in my own spiritual pilgrimage and also in the craft of preparing and preaching the Word by reading both the sermons of others and what many of them have had to say about preaching. I want to share this effort with people that it may accomplish whatever the Spirit wills. In my early ministry I made reading sermons by those who were masters of the art a regular discipline. John Chrysostom, Joseph Parker, John Wesley, Charles Spurgeon, were among the best known in the past. Then Paul Tillich, J.H. Morrison, Gerald Kennedy, Elton Trueblood, Leslie D. Weatherhead, Harry Emerson Fosdick, to mention but a few. I took careful note of the style, the illustrative material, the way the Bible was used and the theological insights which were applied. But I knew too that merely to try and imitate any of these great preachers of the past would be disastrous. If a preacher is not being genuinely herself or himself when she/he preaches, then their basic integrity is in jeopardy. I have been, at times, absolutely thrilled as I listened to preachers like Dr. C.M. (Big Nick) Nicholson. I have never prayed "God help me to preach like that." I knew that only Big Nick could preach like that. But I have prayed that I might put into my preaching the same kind of work, passion, insight and diligence which he did so that I might apply it to the way God wanted me to preach.

I've heard people say: "What we need is another John Wesley." The truth is that John Wesley in our day might be a complete anomaly. What we need in our day is people who will allow the Holy Spirit free rein in their lives as John Wesley did in his, who will allow the same passion for truth and justice to motivate them as it did him. Clones of John Wesley we do not want. What we both need and want are preachers empowered by the Spirit of the living God, committed to truth, as God has revealed it and who will apply it to the issues of our times as John Wesley did to his. We will have them if we are prepared to undergo the discipline and pay the price. Let me quote Dr. C.M. Nicholson at this point. "Jesus came preaching and I do hold the opinion that in a Church like the United Church of Canada we have no option but to take the preaching of the Word of God out of Holy Scripture most seriously."

As I begin this brief paragraph of thanks to people who have helped — a host of faces loom before me. They range from mission fields in the Maritimes and Saskatchewan, to congregations in Cape Breton, New Brunswick and Toronto where I was pastor and from hundreds of congregations across the land where people listened to these words and gave much encouragement to me. I am humbled by their patience, support and appreciation. In addition to my wife and family to whom reference is made in the dedication, two other persons stand out in my memory with deep gratitude. They are "George D", as he was known, and Estella MacDonald — my parents. Perhaps even now in a spiritual sense they are looking down — or over — and smiling that quiet smile they always did when they wanted to say to any one of their children in the Maritime jargon: "Y'done well!"

Deep appreciation goes to my friend Hugh McCullum for his generously worded forword to this book. I feel a kindred spirit when I read his monthly "Observations" and catch the sense of his passion, commitment and dedication to Christ as a living, vibrant spirit waiting to possess the Church.

I am grateful to my friends and former colleagues, Mary O'Keefe and Leone McKinney who with extreme graciousness arranged for and did the typing of the original manuscripts. As well, thanks to Bill Park, Director of CANEC Publishing who from the first mention of this project gave his expertise unstintingly to see it through. Included in that also are the people at CANEC who work at those word processors and computers that almost frighten me.

So, I let these sermons go, wherever they may, with the prayer I frequently offer before preaching:

> May the words of this sermon
> answer questions in the minds of some,
> may they stir up questions in the minds of others.
> And when they are finished
> may none of us be satisfied
> with either the sermon or ourselves.

Thanks be to God.

Clarke MacDonald,
Toronto, Ontario
January 1987.

FOREWORD TO BOOK OF
CLARKE MacDONALD'S SERMONS

When I was reading through these sermons of Clarke MacDonald's I couldn't help recalling something I'd seen on a wall recently in the Philippines. It was in the offices of a Christian human rights agency and it's a quote from Daniel Berrigan:

"Even with the most fervent will, it is not possible for everyone to do everything. We cannot level our lance at every evil, right every wrong. But we can do something, and the moral distance between doing something and doing nothing is momentous indeed."

Clarke MacDonald is a Maritimer. He hasn't lived there for quite a while but at another level he's never left there. He still has that quick quip or fast one-liner that sticks with one long after the incident which sparked that pithy humour has passed.

Clarke would like Berrigan's comment about "the moral distance between doing something and doing nothing...." He might even say, as he sometimes does, "I wish I'd said that." Sometimes he finds out that he "did say that."

A couple of Clarke's sayings that I especially love are mentioned in this book of sermons. One that has become famous is his self-description, "I am an unashamed evangelical and an unrepentant social activist." Another I recall from a Project North meeting when he was United Church representative on that interchurch coalition. He described Christianity as "love with a rib of steel."

There's a great oral tradition among Maritimers. Humour, passion, eloquence, pathos and a rolling-down sense of justice permeate these sermons. They're the direct descendants of those powerful preachers so influenced by the magnificence of their homeland and the struggles of its people to regain their rightful place within Canada.

When Clarke MacDonald starts to tell you about a C'Bretoner down at the pier in Sydney, you never know whether you're going to laugh uproariously or walk away a little wiser and more challenged — probably both.

But this man from Pictou County whose life was shaped by family, by church, by environment, is more than just an eloquent speaker. He's a man of unique compassion, with the sensitivity to suffer with others. He's capable of strong righteous indignation when he sees injustice anywhere. He speaks with blunt outrage at the exploitation of the weak by the strong. He has time for the individual. He is a person of almost awesome integrity. And, I guess for me, above all other things, he's a do-er. He doesn't just talk well, he *does* well.

When he was Moderator of the United Church he went into the prisons when his church expressed support for victims of that dreadful system we maintain. He went to South Africa and came back and picketed with others in front of the consulate. He called apartheid a sin and crime against God and humanity before his church ever declared it a heresy. He stood outside the Litton Industry plant in Rexdale in bitter cold and worshipped the God of Peace with a small group of people who believed deeply that we are called to be peace and justice-makers.

I don't want this man to sound like some paragon that is slightly more than human. He's not. He's deeply human with all the frailties and contradictions that implies but he is also a person who can graciously — and gracefully — listen to others and to other viewpoints.

These sermons are little nuggets of Clarke MacDonald's wisdom and humour and compassion. What you see is what you get. There's the prophet and the pastor; the evangelical and the activist; the human and the divine.

I write this foreword as an invitation to all who read

this book to help themselves to the beauty and challenge of a man of action and a child of God.

Hugh McCullum
Toronto, Ont.
July, 1986.

DON'T STOP THE WORLD — WE HAVE A JOB TO DO

Some of us find a tremendous challenge in those words of Dr. George MacLeod of Iona, Scotland:

"I simply argue that the Cross be raised again at the centre of the market place as well as on the steeple of the Church. I am recovering the claim that Jesus was not crucified in a Cathedral between two candles, but on a Cross between two thieves; on the town garbage heap; on a crossroads so cosmopolitan they they had to write his title in Hebrew and Latin and in Greek (or shall we say in English, in Bantu, and in Afrikaans); at the kind of place where cynics talk smut, and thieves curse, and soldiers gamble. Because that is where He died and that is what He died about. And that is where churchmen should be and what churchmen should be about."

"What matters is not who talks loudest about "return to the Gospel of Jesus Christ" and "reform according to God's Word", but who acts according to it."

Hans Kung in *Theological Meditations*

"Although Christianity is an "other-worldly" way of living in that it derives its values, its power and ultimate purpose from a source outside this planet it is ... incurably earthly. We must not be surprised, if we embark on the course of following the way of Christ, to find that we are at once challenged by mundane difficulties."

1

DON'T STOP THE WORLD —
WE HAVE A JOB TO DO

Text: When the Son of Man (Christ) comes, will he find faith on the earth?

St. Luke 18:8

A few years ago there was a popular song, "Stop the World I Want to Get Off." It is small wonder that such a song was popular then. That was the era which spawned such things on the international scene as the Biafran tragedy, the Vietnam war, 250,000 women raped in Bangledesh, the Yum Kippur war, the assassination of the Kennedy brothers and Martin Luther King. It witnessed also the drug craze, the Watergate scandal with its subsequent erosion of public confidence, and the God is dead theology with its subsequent erosion of faith. That was the time when we landed a man on the moon but could not deliver a bowl of cereal to a child half way around the earth. Cynicism was elevated to a cause and skepticism almost became a religion. It was the decade of hotlines, hot rods and hot pants! Some felt they could not take it any longer — "Stop the World" they cried, "we want off". My thesis in this sermon is that the world is so beautiful, it has so much potential, there is so much God wants us to do as caretakers of the world that I say "Don't stop the world we have a job to do."

POSITIVES AND NEGATIVES

But the "shadow side" of this world is still with us. Victor Frankyl, the philosopher, says that "meaninglessness"

2

is the mark of this age. This is evident in the increase in suicides, especially among teenagers. Disillusionment and cynicism abound and the uncertainty for the future simply intensifies the impact especially upon our youth. But it is not all bad. Responding at the age of 20 to a statement which I had made about life on a Nova Scotia farm half a century ago, our daughter said, "I wish I had lived back then. Life was so simple, it was so peaceful — it was plain good." I replied, "if you had been a child then you would not be alive at the age of 20." She knew what I meant. At the age of five she had open heart surgery. Without that achievement on the part of medical science her life expectancy would have been nineteen. So everything is not negative. It is true we have produced the nuclear bomb and that has meant hell for some people. But we have also produced the cobalt bomb and that has brought hope to thousands. The laser beam is one of the basic instruments of possible conflict in outer space, but it is also the instrument that has restored sight to blind people.

When I met Captain James Bush in Ottawa on Hiroshima day in 1985, I met a person who gave me hope. Captain Bush was for fifteen years the Captain of a nuclear submarine of the American Navy. I asked him why he gave up a high paying job and a prestigious position with an extremely secure future to join the Peace Research Institute in Washington. He was now spending his time going to and fro across the continent speaking to and encouraging groups of peace workers and those opposed to nuclear war. Captain Bush explained that he came to the realization he had been well taught to do his job as the Captain of a nuclear submarine on which were nuclear missiles capable of delivering the power of many Hiroshimas. "I was good at my job" he said, "and could have remained in it for the rest of my working days. But there was one thing they had not taught me. They did not teach me how to handle the fact that if I received the command to discharge the fire power that was at my finger tips, I could go down in history as the first man to destroy in less than a minute more human beings than anyone had ever done in the history of the human race. They had not taught me how to cope with that and I doubt if you can teach anyone how to do it. That is why I left the American Navy and the service of the Pentagon and am

3

now working for the peace movement." People like Captain Bush are flickering lamps of hope in the darkness and disillusionment of our time.

THE BANKRUPTCY OF EXPERTISE

The failure of most experts to solve the gargantuan problems which we face is our world today is patently apparent. It is as true among theologians and preachers as anyone else. Even religion, or should I say "especially religion" has failed to produce peace of mind or peace in our time. In the area of economics, the military and politics, the same thing is true. If you were to take all the economists of this continent and lay them end to end you wouldn't reach a conclusion! (Neither would you reach one if you did the same thing with the theologians.) Just recently the prestigious Harvard Business School reported that the direction which they had been advocating for American society was a kind of "cul-de-sac". We witnessed this in the last few years with the attacks upon the Canadian Catholic Conference of Bishops and the United Church General Council statements on the economy. The very people who condemn the Bishops and the United Church General Council for their statements on this subject are the ones whose solutions so far have created the problems that made the statements by the church leaders necessary. Technology has emerged in our midst that could save us or suffocate us, it could deliver us or destroy us. But I still say, don't stop the world — we have a job to do.

THE ISSUE IS FAITHFULNESS

Jesus asked his disciples the question, "when the Son of Man comes will He find faith on the earth?" We cannot think of this in terms of some far off divine event. Jesus declared that the Kingdom of God is here. The question He is asking then is since the Kingdom is in our midst and the Christ is in our midst, does He now find us faithful or does He find us in a spirit of rebellion and betrayal. Notice He did not say "When I come will I find piety? Will I find people who keep the ten commandments, go to church, who have all the answers, who are religious?" What he said was "Will I find

4

faith?'' That is will He find people who really trust, who turn over the controls of their lives and their society to the God revealed in Jesus Christ. That's what commitment is all about.

Will He find people who are obedient to the New Testament demands? This will mean some of the above things such as going to church, saying our prayers and keeping the ten commandments. But these are not ends in themselves. They are tools toward serving the higher end of being faithful. We are called to be obedient — we are not called to be popular. We are called to be faithful — we are not called to be successful. And in every one of these issues it is we, not others, who have the responsibility to decide which side will feel the stubborn ounces of our weight.

WHAT ARE PEOPLE SAYING?

The response to these issues in the church and the world is varied. I want to use as illustration of this a few communications which I have received from the church at large. They stand in sharp contrast one to another and indicate both the kind of society in which we live and the kind of community of faith of which we are a part.

1. RESPONSE FROM BUSINESSMEN

The first of these two responses was from a businessman who was protesting against the church's involvement in too many issues. "Why don't you leave politics and economics to the politicians and the economists and stick to religion?" he asked. He went on to criticize the church for its criticism of business and their investments in South Africa. "Don't you know that the trickle down theory helps the blacks more than the kind of boycotts the church is suggesting?" At that time he raised an issue that was common to the work of most of the churches: "Why don't you get off Nestle's back?" he asked, "Aren't they good corporate citizens? And do these medical doctors, pediatricians, missionaries and others really know what they are talking about?" He contended that he considered me to be "a very dangerous person" because I was leading the church to involvement in these issues when we should be "sticking to religion". It was quite obvious that for him to stick

5

to religion meant to be exclusively concerned about the business of "saving souls".

The second letter was also from a businessman but he came across in a very different mood. He said in part, "I am writing this from Florida where I have come to escape from the business world for a while. These Americans are so frustrated with the social and political state of things that they go off on a spiritual odyssey to God. Even now they are talking about the possibility of winning a nuclear war. I am presently struggling with Toffler's book, "The Third Wave". Such an awareness may be clever and enlightening, but what do we do to accelerate the changes and stop the arms race — and move on to the post capitalist era? (And imagine that from a small business entrepreneur.) "Yes, I would enjoy a lunch and talk with you some time when I am in Toronto. We need each other in this lonely world — full of so much reaction, Reaganism and trying to make war fashionable." Thus we find two highly committed business men, both United Church laymen, each taking quite different points of view but supporting his position from what he conceives to be a strong ethical base.

2. TWO DOCTORS SPEAK OUT

And there were letters from two medical doctors. One wrote "The Church in Society mailing came to my attention. I am concerned about all the issues you raise — poverty, unemployment, energy, nuclear power. Especially I am concerned about nuclear development and the possibility of nuclear war." This doctor is a member of Physicians for Social Responsibility and an environmentalist.

The second doctor wrote, "We need to be concerned about how formidable the opposition to human rights is. I need to remind myself of the forces we are up against. This might make some people despondent but it makes others more determined to fight the good fight for a more just and humane world society."

3. TWO WOMEN SPEAK OUT ON
HOMOSEXUALITY

Another letter was from a woman. It was very forth-
right. "I am angry. You preachers speak of the rights of homosexuals. They have no rights except to live decent lives the way
the rest of us do. When they are tempted to sin they should do
as I do and put their trust in God." Her letter echoed another
one which I received about the same time from a man who
said, "I'll tell you what to do with homosexuals — put all of
them in a room, then seal it up so that the air can't get in or
out." He signed himself "a committed layman." He did not say
what he was committed to — I guess it was homicide! Finally
there was a letter from a deeply concerned mother. She wrote,
"I am a mother. Thank you for the letter you and your colleagues had published in the paper about homosexuals. You
said that while you did not approve of the lifestyle of homosexuals you accepted them as persons who have the same human
rights as the rest of us. Yes, I am a mother; my son is a
homosexual. No one will ever know the pain and trauma that
we have gone through together. But I love him very much. He
was so relieved to read your letter. He said, 'Look! these church
leaders are saying that I am a person and I have rights the same
as other people do and all along I have felt the church didn't
care.' " She continued, "he is a good man — he holds a very
prominent position. I can't give you my name or address because you would easily recognize him and I must not betray
him."

THAT'S OUR WORLD AND OUR CHURCH

Well, sisters and brothers, that's the kind of world we
live in and that's the kind of church we worship in whether
we like it or not — and I don't want off — until God calls me
off. We have a job to do. But the question remains, will Christ
find faithfulness when he comes — will He find faithfulness
now as his spirit moves in and out among us, or will He find
people who run for cover, who batten down the hatches and
who stone the prophets, who want to get back to the good old
days. Up, up the moral majority. Jerry Falwell to the rescue
and all that. This is the sort of humanistic triumphalism that

prompted Ronald Reagan to say, "There is nothing wrong with America we can't fix." What has happened to good old-fashioned humility and repentance?

THE TASK BEFORE US

So if we don't want off, then why do we want to stay on and what are we going to do about it?

Surely faithfulness in the midst of the pluralism of our time is one of the primary tasks. The variety of interpretations about life and its meaning which exists even within the church means that we must learn to live with the differences, and at the same time strive to maintain our own integrity. Ours is not a monolithic society or monolithic church. Such a society would be one where everyone held to the same ideology and moved in some kind of locked step toward their goal. Canada used to be to a large extent, a 'bilithic' society. That is, it was French and English — Roman Catholic and Protestant. It is so no longer. It is indeed what the historian called "a mosaic". It is not a block of one colour or shade, or ideological, theological, or cultural position. There are more Muslims in Canada than there are Presbyterians, and Christians are a minority on the planet earth. And what a delightful mix we have in the United Church! In the United Church we have quiet Christians and verbose ones; we have people who want to withdraw and pray and people who want to trust and get involved; we have charismatic evangelical Christians and avante garde liberals and social activists. This is both our strength and our weakness. It is our winsomeness to some and repulsiveness to others. It is our beauty and our ugliness. It is our health and our affliction. It is also the quality that gives me a love for my church, because it is big enough to contain all this diversity. But it can only be maintained if there is a respect for each other. I only have a right to say, "Don't stop the world I have got a job to do," if I am prepared to make room in that world for the brother or sister who differs from me, but is prepared to live in peace and fairness with me. I want to be faithful in the midst of all this.

NO TIDY PACKAGE

If I wanted a church which had a tidy little package of beliefs all neatly wrapped with the ribbons of orthodoxy, stamped with some kind of good housekeeping seal of approval of infallible doctrine and delivered as an immaculate expression of absolute truth — then I would not look to the United Church of Canada. But if I wanted a church where people have convictions but were nevertheless open to people with different viewpoints, where they believed in freedom in obedience, in the acceptance of people but not necessarily in the acceptance of everything they say and do, that to apply the faith is more important than to preserve it, then I would say the United Church is my kind of church. Beware of the church which glibly says, "We have all the answers." Beware of the church which glibly says in a simplistic way, "Christ is the answer." But take seriously the church which says, "The answer is to be found in Christ; finding it and working out the implications of it is a lifetime vocation."

I do not believe in going around bad mouthing the church. (There are enough people doing that without me adding my words.) This does not mean I approve of everything that is said and done by my church or any other. Of course the church has its faults and weaknesses and I could spend a lot of time talking about them and analysing them. So had the church at Corinth, Galatia, Ephesus and Thessalonica. Make a list of the things about which those churches were concerned and compare them with the things about which the churches are concerned today and see the similarity.

Concerns of the New Testament Church
1. They were concerned about good news and praise to God.
2. They were concerned about the rights of women, children, slaves, foreigners and others.

3. In Jerusalem they took a collection for the poor and the church sought to fulfil the commandment of Christ's "Inasmuch as you do it to these you do it to me."

Concerns of the Churches Today
1. We are concerned about evangelism and worship.
2. We are concerned about human rights in El Salvador, in Poland, South Africa, the Middle East and in Canada.
3. We claim the option of solidarity with the poor.

9

4. They were concerned about moral issues, temperance and profanity.	4. We are concerned about the moral issues of intemperance, fraud, pornography.
5. They asserted that God is no respecter of person.	5. We are concerned about the worth of every human being on the planet Earth.

So they said and so we say, "Don't stop the world, we have a job to do." This first of all then, faithfulness to the truth as we understand it, with charity toward those of a different understanding. As John Wesley said, "In matters of theological interpretation I think and I let think, if your heart is as my heart then give me your hand." We are called to be obedient, we are not necessarily called to be successful; we are called to be faithful, we are not necessarily called to be popular.

THE FAITHFULNESS OF RESPONSE

If the church is going to be faithful in response then it is going to run risks. Sometimes the church is in trouble with various kinds of establishment powers. It is probably never more like Jesus than in such a situation. If the time ever comes that the United Church is out of trouble, then I am going to join a church that is in trouble — because that is where the church ought to be and that's what faithfulness is about. One of our former Moderators, Dr. Lois Wilson, when in Korea asked the question, "What is the difference between the Jesus Church of Korea and the Christ Church of Korea?" She got the answer, "If you believe in the Jesus Church you go to heaven — if you believe in the Christ Church you go to prison." She observed and I can only applaud the observation, why can't we have it both ways? Why can we not have room for the involvement of our churches in Canada with the charismatic as well as the activist, the avante garde liberal as well as the evangelical? This, of course, is going to demand a strong effort to respect the integrity and the rights of others. It is worth observing that the divisions which exist in the church in Korea today between the Jesus Church and the Christ Church were the result of the exportation of our own rigid denominationalism and fundamentalism. Now the chickens have come home to roost.

PARTICIPATION

Archbishop Oscar Romero was not shot in El Salvador at the Holy Table because he was conducting the Eucharist. He was shot because the day before he had gone out on the street and identified himself with the plight of the poor and the peasants, especially the wives, mothers and sisters of the disappeared. Martin Luther King was not shot in Memphis, Tenn. because the night before he had made his famous speech, "I have been to the mountain top, I have a dream, my eyes have seen the glory of the coming of the Lord and I am not afraid to die." He was shot because he dared to stand shoulder to shoulder with the black garbage collectors — in that society the lowest form of human experience one could imagine. Thus, Romero linked the Holy Table to the act of walking with the peasants and the poor. Martin Luther King linked his dream with the need to be involved in the dusty and sweaty and profane world of garbage collectors. It is a reflection or echo of Rabbi Martin Buber's statement, "Religion begins in awe and ends in politics." The churches can no longer be content just to pick up the pieces after other forces have gone through and decimated human beings, deprived them of their rights and taken from them their dignity. Because we see, as Mother Theresa has said, the face of Christ in the welfare mother, the unemployed, the tortured, we must do more than pick up the pieces. We must try to prevent the pieces from happening.

LET ME TELL YOU ABOUT JOSE

"Jose was 18 months old when the men in uniform pushed long steel needles under his fingernails, as his father, broken and bloody, looked on.

It was a means of making the father talk. Too bad he had nothing to tell.

The scene was a regional military headquarters in Chile in 1974, a dull, one-storey concrete block which still houses a modern-day chamber of horror.

Jose was playing with friends on the road outside his house when they took him to "visit his daddy" in jail.

Today, thousands of miles away, he is six years old and he is with his daddy again.

But he doesn't play with other children. In the kindergarten, he sits alone in corners, saying nothing. When the voice of the others playing becomes too much, he escapes to the toilet and crouches there, eyes shut tight, hands over his ears, trying to blot it out."

You don't have to be a flaming radical or a left wing nut of some kind before you want to say in the face of that sort of thing — knowing that it is happening in fifty nations around the world — "In the name of the Lord God Jehovah — stop!"

PERSONAL FAITHFULNESS

The third thing we need to ask ourselves in response to the question when Christ comes will he find faith on the earth is the intensely personal question, "Will he find us to be faithful? Will he find faithfulness in Canada? Will he find faithfulness in this congregation? Will he find faithfulness in John and Mary Christian? Will he find faithfulness in Clarke MacDonald? (Put your own name in there and ask yourself the same question.)

It boils down to the question that Jesus asked three times of Peter when he passed to him the responsibility of being a pastor. Three times Jesus asked, "Simon Peter lovest thou me?" The Gospel writer must have overheard this conversation because he says, "Peter was grieved that the Lord asked him the third time, lovest thou me?" We need to see this incident in the light of Peter's three times denying in Caiaphus' judgment hall that he even knew who Jesus was. Recall that on that occasion he went out and wept bitterly because he let down his friend and his master. We should also weep. We should also expect to hear, not only three but thirty-three times the question, lovest thou me? When we fail as we will, we will find our hope and renewed strength where Peter found his. "Blessed be the God and Father of our Lord Jesus Christ, who has begotten us again to a living hope by the resurrection of Jesus Christ from the dead." In that strength and hope we go on in this world not wanting off, not wanting to get out from our responsibilities, but to say in the time honoured words, "Here am I Lord, use me."

Thanks be to God. Amen.

A FAITH FOR TOUGH TIMES

Concerning faith —

Notes picked up in passing:

1. "Faith is the working principle of daily life."

2. "I do not believe in any creed, but I use creeds to express, to conserve, and to deepen my belief in God."

Archbishop Wm. Temple.

3. "We should doubt our doubts before we doubt our beliefs."

4. "There lies more faith in honest doubt believe me than in half the creeds."

5. A little boy returned from fishing and a friend asked: "Did you catch many fish today?" The boy replied: "I didn't catch as many as I hoped to, but then I really didn't think I would."

6. Faith is a continuous journey with points of arrival on the way. (From this sermon.)

A FAITH FOR TOUGH TIMES

Text: "This is the victory that overcomes the world
even our faith."

St.John.

ONLY A TOUGH FAITH DESERVES TO SURVIVE

Elie Weisel, the Hebrew philosopher and poet, as well
as the teenage survivor of the Holocaust, said: "It is harder to
believe in God than not to believe in God."

Only a tough faith will survive, or deserves to survive
in our time. By this I do not mean a macho, arrogant and
imperialistic spirituality. We are still trying to recover from the
aftermath of that approach. We know the power of faith as
small as a grain of grass seed or like the silent powerful yeast
hidden in dough. We've seen a tree defiant, stubborn, growing
out of the crevice of a rock on some bleak and barren slope.
That seedling was probably healthier and tougher than the one
which produced a spreading chestnut in some shady, fertile
valley. Likewise, it may take more faith to be a devoted and
diligent parent to a son or daughter who has gotten embroiled
in all sorts of deviation from accepted social or moral norms,
than to be the parent of the proper youth who does all the right
things for the right reasons.

As Janet Somerville wrote on the "Back Page" of the
Observer: "We are most truly open to the paschal mystery of
dying and rising when we are in situations beyond our strength,

beyond even our capacity to understand or to love."[1]

But back a moment to Elie Weisel's comment: "It is harder to believe in God than not to believe." He no doubt said that against the background of the trauma of Auschwitz and the torture and the death camp. But it is also true in our less intense scenes. If I say I do not believe in God, then except for some humanistic impulse that I probably got from the community of faith in the first place, I have no need to pay attention to any of the demands and precepts of the faith — of any faith. I may choose to care about my neighbour but I am not obligated by faith to do so. I may choose to speak the truth out of self interest but I could without a blush tell a lie and feel no compunction about it. I may choose to "love peace and pursue it" as the psalmist said, but on the other hand I may without regret follow the way of violence and retaliation. I may choose to "do justice, love mercy and walk humbly with God," as the prophet exhorts, or I may choose to defy God, to walk in arrogance — without humility and loving revenge while eschewing mercy.

QUALITY OF FAITH MAKES THE DIFFERENCE

This is precisely the point I want to make. Faith ought to make a difference and if it's a tough enough faith it will make a difference. I have yet to meet a thorough going atheist. Sceptics — yes, they come a dime a dozen. Agnostics — yes, people want proof before they believe. They are numerous. But atheists — no. By virtue of the fact that they put themselves and their ideas up as being the ultimate word in the interpretation of the universe and the meaning of life, they usurp the place of God. They become God! They have not ceased to believe. They have simply shifted the focus of their belief from a somewhat objective reality to themselves. They become the sum of all that is.

Walking by the Red Square in Moscow one day with a young guide and interpreter on my way to meet the Director of Religious Affairs of the Politburo of the USSR, I saw a lineup of people, many of them young people, three blocks long walking slowly four abreast. Some were carrying flowers and all of

---

1. March 1986.

them paused momentarily at Lenin's tomb to pay their respects, deposit their flowers, or in some subtle way almost genuflect before this great leader's tomb. When I met the Director of Religious Affairs an hour later, his first question was, "What do you think of the USSR?" "Oh," I replied, "I perceive among other things that your people are very religious." "Religious," he almost shouted, "What do you mean religious?" "Well," I said, "as I passed by Lenin's tomb I saw hundreds of young people and others lined up paying homage to Mr. Lenin. To me that was a form of worship." "O, they were not paying homage," he replied, "they were just saying thank you to the father of the fatherland." Well, I did not pursue the matter further because I had other things to discuss with him such as the human rights of the dissident Sakarov and the release of Scharinsky, who was then in prison, as well as the right of the Jews to emigrate from the USSR. But I think the incident bore out the truth of my previous statement — "they usurp the place of God."

FAITH AS CONTINUOUS SEARCH AND ARRIVAL

What I am driving at here is the notion that my faith after all is the final truth on which I anchor life. To protest that such truth does not exist does not relieve me of the business of living and somewhere my mind will either come to rest on what I accept as being that ultimate truth or it will tortuously pursue the realization of it. It is a case of being on a continuing journey with intermittent way stations. If I reject all affirmations of objective reality then It, or He, or She, if we perceive the ultimate reality in personal terms, becomes a creation of my own mind. God in the final analysis is that Being, Thing, Spirit or Essence which means more to us than anything else and on which all our values ultimately rest. Anything or anyone can become your God. Name it and you can deify it. Some people make a god out of the Bible, or out of a Creed, or a Church, or a political party, or money or their club. One's race or nation can become one's god. Sex, politics, money, position, national pride and tradition, can and sometimes do become our idol.

"THE LEAP OF FAITH."

The proposition I advance to you is that I prefer to take the "leap of faith" and accept, not with an uncritical mind, what has been tested in the Judeo-Christian faith for over 3,000 years, than to set up a puny system of belief created by Clarke MacDonald — even if it were done in consultation with the most erudite minds of our time. My faith then is rooted and grounded in the revelation — the showing forth — of God's love and grace in the Prophets and in Jesus Christ. As such it is ever growing, expanding, surprised by what God has in store around the next corner.

It is indeed a tough time for faith and we need a tough faith to be equal to these times. There is a broad sense of alienation, frustration and loneliness even in the area of faith and its understanding. This has created, especially on the part of some young people, a sense of cynicism and even of fear. The accumulated social deficits of two world wars and a major depression, the fall-out from two decades of a burgeoning, acquisitive and materialistic society, along with leadership that seems hell-bent on computerizing the planet into destruction in ten years or less probably accounts for the fact that attempted suicides are up 300 percent, and suicide amongst teenagers in Canada is the highest on record. It may be worth our while to look at some of the characteristics of a faith that will be adequate to the time in which we live. You may identify with some of these characteristics or your participation in preaching at this moment may prompt you to think of other aspects of a faith tough enough to meet your situation.

INTELLECTUAL HONESTY

First a faith for tough times must be intellectually honest. An adequate faith is one that has intellectual integrity. By this I do not mean one has to have a string of degrees after one's name to possess it. Some of the most intelligent people I have met had only a grade 8 education my own father, for instance. On the other hand some of the dumbest people I have known .... well, let's skip that! What I mean here is that I don't want to be like the young man who went to College and, after getting a few courses in philosophy under his belt, wrote to his father and said, "At last I have become an atheist — thank God!" We need to recall that it was Jesus who expanded the Old Testament exhortation about love of God to include the mind. The Old Testament says, "Thou shalt love the Lord thy God with all thy heart, with all thy strength, and with all thy soul." Jesus said, "Thou shalt love the Lord thy God with all thy heart, strength, soul and *mind.*" I visited a Muslim mosque recently and there was a sign at the door, "Please leave your shoes outside." Some people, so it seems, would almost put a sign outside the door of the church that read, "Please leave your minds outside!" We are to love God with all our minds as well as with other parts of our being. Faith is a kind of spiritual muscle with mental sinews. I checked that analogy out with a medical doctor and he tells me it is adequate. A muscle without sinews cannot enable you to walk, run or lift a burden. Sinews without muscle are also useless. A faith that is comprised of spiritual muscle and mental sinews can enable you to journey on the tough terrain of today's world. Do not be afraid when, in this testing, doubts assail your mind. God may be nearer to you at the point of doubt than at any other.

A MEANINGFUL ENCOUNTER IN SOUTH AFRICA

When in South Africa recently, one of the high moments was visitations with people who are waging, at great personal sacrifice, a battle against the iniquitous notion of apartheid — the separation of people on the basis of race and colour. One of these persons was Cedric Mayson, a former minister of the Methodist Church, who had joined the Christian Institute, now a banned organization, and then formed the Institute of Contextual Theology which also has recently been banned. Cedric was in prison for fifteen months because of his convictions and his public elaboration of them. During that time he spent five months in solitary confinement. For a period of seventy-two hours he was forced to stay awake, not allowed to lie down or to sit down, provided limited food, some of his hair was pulled out, his faith was mocked and he was otherwise abused. At the end of that time as he put it, "My mind was so befogged and my will so shattered that when they put a piece of paper in front of me I signed it." It is to the credit of the judiciary of

South Africa that, when he was on trial, the judge threw out this piece of evidence as being unallowable because it had been extracted from him under duress. He was released on 1,000 rand bail the day we arrived in South Africa. When we returned to Canada, along with other concerned Christians in Toronto and Ottawa, vigils were arranged outside of the South African Consulate and the South African Embassy in which prayers were offered for Cedric Mayson, Bishop Tutu, Bayers Naudes and others. Even as we were on our way to this vigil, we received word from International News Service that Cedric Mayson had escaped from South Africa through Lesotho across to Mozambique and was now in London, England.

As we sat in the living room of their home in Johannesburg with Cedric and his wife, Penelope, Cedric was telling us about his understanding of liberation theology. He said, "It isn't just liberation in general terms we need to think of. It must be specific. It's liberation of Blacks, liberation of native people, liberation of women .... it has to zero in somewhere. The supreme liberation, of course," he added, "was the liberation which Jesus experienced on the Cross when he cried out, 'My God, my God, why hast thou foresaken me?' and in that moment of feeling most foresaken he was also most assured of God's nearness and presence and he was able to say 'Father, into thy hands I commit my Spirit.' " When Cedric said that, his voice broke and tears welled into his eyes. "That," he said, "was what sustained me during the lonely hours in prison." A faith like that is not blind acceptance of anything. Neither is it guesswork. It is staking your life on a given proposition ... but a proposition that was fully revealed in a person. It is not mere acquiescence to a credal statement. It has nothing to do with dead dogma. It means commitment to a person, in this case the Person of Jesus Christ and to the things for which He stood — and stands. The road to this understanding of faith is sometimes fraught with pain and peril. Let us not give up on the journey but realize as someone put it, "There lies more faith in honest doubt, believe me, than in half the Creeds.

PROCLAIMER OF FAITH — NOT PROVER OF A PROPOSITION

We are not then the provers of a proposition. I did not prepare this sermon to prove to you there is a God. I prepared it to proclaim a faith — the faith that at the heart of things — of all things — there is a Being, a Spirit, a Power, an Essence, and in my script every one of those words Being, Spirit, Power, Essence begins with a capital letter — because I believe this power is also awesome and worthy of our worship and fully revealed in Jesus Christ. As we put it in a contemporary Creed, "We are not alone, we live in God's world ... we are not alone. In life, in death, in life beyond death, God is with us."

OBVIOUS LIMITATIONS

Now I would be the first to admit the limits of this approach through the mind. The limitations are fairly obvious. Karl Barth had one of the most prodigious minds ever to address itself to the interpretation of Christian truth. There is a story which I am assured is not apocryphal that when he was dying someone asked him if he had any "final words" out of all his reading and reflecting which in that hour he wanted to share with posterity. He is alleged to have said that he did. Can't you sense the eagerness with which people would wait for him to reply, and what did they hear? "Yes," the great theologian replied, "I want to leave a final word with them. It is this: 'Jesus loves me, this I know.' " Sometimes we hesitate to sing that hymn because we think it is rather childish, yet here was one of the greatest theological minds of this century coming to rest at precisely this point, "Jesus loves me, this I know."

EMOTIONAL ADEQUACY

This leads us naturally into the next point I want to make, which is that a faith for tough times must not only be intellectually honest, but it must be emotionally adequate. Emotionalism in religion, if allowed to run riot, can be a devastating and damaging thing. Absence of it totally can leave us with a cold and sterile mixture. Religion without passion is like the bagpipes without wind, beautiful to look at but never stirring the blood or moving the feet. Our spirits, like our bodies, need a balanced diet or they get out of kilter. They may become constipated with an overlay of intellectualism, or diarrhetic with a surfeit of sentimentalism and emotionalism. When that happens there is no kind of spiritual epsom salts you can take to give you instant relief! You need the prescription laid down in Galilee 2,000 years ago; it is still valid, "Love God with all your *heart*, strength, soul and mind and your neighbour as yourself." When emotionalism gets out of hand, it produces the sort of picture I saw of a Jehovah Witness woman standing white-knuckled, gripping the foot of her child's bed in the hospital, and saying over and over again as she refused to give her child a blood transfusion, "It is the will of God — it is the will of God." Nonsense! It was not the will of God. It was the will of a woman whose mind had been trapped by an arrogant, fundamentalist theology.

TRAGEDY OF EMOTIONALISM RUN RIOT

It is emotionalism that produces a Jonesville with all its tragedy. It cons people into borrowing money to support the electronic evangelists — some of whom are charlatans of the airways. Such people impair the work being done by preachers like Billy Graham, through their spiritualistic Amway approach. What I am pleading for here is a balance. So I am assuming a balance between intellectual and emotional adequacy. The emotional factor is part of our human makeup. To ignore it is folly, to over accentuate it can be disastrous. The assertion that Canadians are not an emotional people is not borne out by attendance at or reaction to a hockey game, the Grey Cup or other such events. I know people who even get emotional over the Blue Jays — or is it the Expos! The feeling component in our religious experience while indefinable, is significant. Whether it is Jesus weeping over Jerusalem, Paul's tears at Ephesus, the outpouring of Monica, the mother of Augustine, the "strange warm feeling in my heart", experienced by Wesley, or Martin Luther King saying a moment before he was shot, "I am not afraid to die, I have been to the mountain top and mine eyes have seen the glory of the coming of the Lord and I am not afraid to die." We need to see not only the value but also how important a component emotion is in a tough faith approach. Those whom I just named, through whose veins there coursed the corpuscles of love and who never allowed the arteries of compassion to harden, have set for us a model and we need a positive response. This movement of the spirit is not in defiance of mind but it is more than intellectual assent. It is an act of the will and that implies feeling and willing, as well as knowing.

EFFECTIVE INVOLVEMENT

The final factor in this equation of faith is effective involvement. People shy away from this today. They do more than shy away from it, they denounce it and imply it is a waste of time. When a Pakistani was attacked on the Toronto subway by a bunch of racists, those who looked on and did nothing said, "We didn't want to get involved." When people saw a woman gang-raped in an American restaurant, they looked on, laughing, jeering and refusing to get involved in the woman's protection. On the other side of the ledger, when a man defended a black person from an attack and suffered two broken legs as a consequence, he explained his action to Roy Bonisteel by saying, "When I see someone being attacked because of the colour of their skin, I just can't help getting involved and I would do it again." When Samantha Smith wrote Yuri Andropov, in response to which she received an invitation from the Soviet leader to visit "our vast and beautiful country", she was ready to be involved. When the United Church in the British Columbia Conference decided to send the Mission boat Crosby V down through the straits of Juan du Fuca and through Puget Sound to the Trident missile base at Bangor, Washington, it was getting involved in the peace issue. When I stood on the deck of the Crosby the morning we arrived in the most shrouded mountain region of Washington State and I thought of this little mission boat going out to meet the Trident, which is the size of two football fields and carries within it the equivalent of 2,040 Hiroshima bombs, I thought of the words of St. Paul, "The weak things of the world shall confound the mighty."

THE CHURCH DARE NOT BACK OFF

So when people write me letters telling me to back off the peace issue, when they tell me that the United Church had no business getting involved in the fate of prisoners at Archambault or anywhere else, or that we should forget about human rights in South Africa, South Korea and South America, or forget about Canada's native people and "stick to religion", I have to say "I am sorry but it cannot be so." The Church cannot sit up in the gallery of life and look down on the arena where men and women are working and playing, sweating and swearing, laughing and weeping, birthing and dying. 'It must get down in the arena of life and be involved. Involvement always implies the element of risk. But is this not what faith is ultimately about — risk?

THE SPIRITUAL CORD THAT BINDS

Finally, that which holds these three features of a tough faith — intellectual honesty, emotional adequacy and effective involvement in healthy tension is, for me, meaningful worship and disciplined prayer life.

On a Sunday morning in February, 1983, my wife and I arrived in Johannesburg. We were taken to St. Paul's Anglican Church in Soweto, to the service of Holy Communion. We were two of about six white people among nearly 1,000 blacks who were present. I was not aware it was a Communion Service until just toward the end of it when a friendly helpful black woman, who had been sitting next to us and had been interpreting the Afrikanner sections of the service, indicated to us that they were now entering the part which was the Sacrament of Holy Communion. I usually like to go to a Holy Communion service knowing that I am doing so and having made certain mental and spiritual preparations for that experience. So when she turned to me and said, "Are you going to make your Communion?", with typical western caution I said, "I am not sure." She waited a few moments and then looked at me with deep penetrating eyes framed against her strong black countenance and said, "Well — are you ready to make your Communion?" I said, "Yes, I am ready." I went slowly up the aisle with the people moving toward the Holy Table and said within myself, "Lord, I am not ready, but I am as ready as I ever will be." As I knelt to receive the sacrament with my black sisters and brothers and a white priest offered me the bread, "the body of Christ broken for you," and a black priest offered me the wine, "the Blood of Christ shed for you," I never felt myself more a part of the total stream of God's people or God's purpose than I did in that moment.

So from this black woman, whose name I do not know — to our church — I pass the challenge, "Are we ready?" Are we ready mentally — with intellectual integrity; emotionally — with passion; and practically — with effective involvement to take up our Cross and follow Christ? That is where a tough faith should lead us in a tough time.

Thanks be to God. Amen.

BOTH SIDES NOW

"I am an unashamed evangelical and an unrepentant social activist."

"At the heart of the Church there has always been the breaking of bread, and when the sacrament is divorced from the dream of a Christian social order it is deprived of its significance. If we cut off the Bread which is His body from all connection with our daily bread — if we declare that He is present in the Bread of the Sanctuary but absent from the Bread in the Street, we deny the truth of the Incarnation ....." (Studdert Kennedy)

"Social activity is a consequence of evangelism."
"Social activity can be a bridge to evangelism."
"Social activity is a partner in evangelism."

(World Evangelical Fellowship — Lausanne Committee.)

BOTH SIDES NOW
(A SPIRITUAL BASIS FOR
SOCIAL ACTION)

Scriptures — St. Matthew 17: 1-21

INTRODUCTION

I am an unashamed evangelical and an unrepentant social activist. In other words I do not believe that we have a social gospel and an individual gospel, or that pietism is enough on the one hand and activism is enough on the other. This duality may be called the two sides of the same coin. If you have a Canadian dime (equal to about a Canadian nickel in 1961 currency) with a picture of the Bluenose on one side and the value of ten inscribed on the other, you have legitimate currency. If the dime had either the Bluenose or the value of ten erased or never put on it, then it would not pass as legitimate currency and you could not buy anything with it. Likewise, a Christian life that is all go, go, activism — do this, do that, go there, protest here — and that never touches the depths of spiritual reality or reflects on what Rudolph Otto called the "holy other", does not witness to the wholeness of the Gospel. On the other hand, a faith that is all pietism, prayers, hymn singing, "brother I am saved" and that glosses over the evils of society — never protests against them — never rebukes the perpetrators of them — is likewise half a gospel. What you end up with here is a truncated faith, not the Gospel of our Lord Jesus Christ. A "full Gospel" is just that, the fullness of the Gospel in its personal and social dimension. It is a Gospel filled not just with the Holy Spirit but filled with a Holy Spirit that issues in a practical application of the Gospel or else the Holy Spirit has not done its task of filling.

It is interesting that one of the greatest "put-downs" some people feel they can direct to a Christian today is to say that he or she is a "do-gooder". This is interesting because this is precisely what St. Stephen said about Jesus. In giving his account of Jesus in the only sermon he ever preached, and for which he was stoned to death, St. Stephen recounted the many great and wonderful things which Jesus achieved in his ministry, and he tucked in this innocent little phrase, "Jesus went about doing good." "I cannot praise", said John Milton, "a cloistered and sequestered virtue that is afraid to sally forth." Neither can I commend a faith that is closeted, unwilling to get involved, and which interprets the words "keep yourself unspotted from the world," as meaning "don't get involved in the world."

BASIC — EVANGELICAL — LIBERAL — ACTIVIST

The night I was elected Moderator, in Montreal on August 9, 1982, I spent a couple of hours with the media people. One reporter said something like, "There exists a lot of tension in the church today between various theological positions. They range from right wing conservatives to left wing avant garde activists. Where do you stand on this?" I replied, "You can put me down as being a basic, evangelical, liberal activist!" He looked at me as much as to say, "What kind of a quadra-headed monster is that?" As I reflect on it, I do not disavow the statement. I have also met a number of ministers since that time who tell me they were very encouraged by those words. I know we have to use labels because of the limitations of language to express the wholeness of truth. But I dislike it when those labels are stuck out front as badges that pretend to tell everything about us. If you say, "Clarke MacDonald is a Maritimer" you speak the truth — but not the whole truth. He is also a Canadian, a citizen of the global community — a member of the human race, and a Christian. What I meant by the phrase "basic, evangelical, liberal activist", was this. Basic, because my faith is based on a biblical, theological foundation centering on the revelation of God in Jesus Christ our Lord. Evangelical, because I have a faith I want to share with others. Liberal, because I respect the opinion of those who differ from me in these matters (and I expect them to respect mine). And finally activist, because I do not believe the church can sit up in the gallery of life and look down on the world where men and women are working and playing and sweating and swearing, and laughing and weeping and birthing and dying — it must be down there involved in that world. But more of this later.

THE BIBLICAL SETTING

Let us look now for a little while at the story in St. Matthew 17: 1-21. This story appears in St. Matthew and must have been told to him or at least received directly or indirectly from either Peter, James or John. You know it well but let me remind you of its outline. Jesus had been at Caesarea Phillipi, where Peter made his great confession of Him as "the Christ, the Son of the living God." Six days later with apparent cool deliberation and intention, Jesus went up a mountain with Peter, James and John. On that mountain something substantially different from any natural phenomenon they had ever experienced took place. It was transcendental, mysterious, eerie — some people would say almost scary. It appeared to the disciples that Jesus was talking with Moses and Elijah, the great among the Hebrew prophets. There is no record of the nature or content of that conversation. But they were so sure it was a fact that Peter made a proposal to structure it. Isn't it interesting that whenever a prophet appears on the scene we want to institutionalize the prophet! We want to build something that will confine the experience to a given place and a given time.

OLD TESTAMENT SIMILARITY

It is interesting that this experience has a kindred account in the Old Testament. In Exodus 24: 12-18, you have the account of Moses responding to the Lord's invitation to go up on the mountain top and wait there until he received the law and the commandments. Moses also took a friend named Joshua with him. The children of Israel were left at the foot of the mountain. We read, "Then Moses went up on the mountain, and the cloud covered the mountain. The glory of the

Lord settled on Mt. Sinai .... now the appearance of the glory of the Lord was like a devouring fire on the top of the mountain in the sight of the people of Israel." It is interesting to trace the treatment of this occasion since that time. What Moses received on the mountain top was the law and the commandments summarized in what the Hebrew people to this day refer to as the "Torah". In the Jewish synagogue of our time the Torah is kept in the Ark of the Covenant, which is erected at a high point of prominence at the front of the synagogue.

I remember preaching one Friday night in a synagogue in Toronto. After the psalms, the prayers, the scriptures, and the sermon, there came the high moment in the service. The elders in the congregation slowly and reverently approached the Ark of the Covenant. They opened the doors and revealed the Torah to the people. Immediately as they did so there was the sound of trumpets (interestingly enough in this synagogue the trumpeter that night was a member of the Church Army of the Anglican Church) and the people raised their voices in a shout of praise and thanksgiving to God. They were celebrating the remembrance of the time God delivered them from slavery in Egypt. They were praising God that "God the Lord is one." As I reflected on this experience, it occurred to me that in our service of Christian witness when the minister presiding at the Holy Table during the Eucharist breaks the bread "my body broken for you", and raises the cup "my blood shed for you", we should have a blast of trumpets and a shout of praise because this is the moment of our deliverance.

That would seem to be what Jesus was trying to communicate here and even as Peter reflected upon it when he wrote his second letter to the churches, referring to his own imminent departure, he said, "For we did not follow cleverly devised myths when we made known to you the power and coming of our Lord Jesus Christ, but we were eyewitnesses of his majesty. For when he received honour and glory from God the Father and the voice was borne to him by the majestic glory, "This is my beloved Son with whom I am well pleased," we heard this voice borne from heaven, *for we were with him on the holy mountain.* So it is small wonder that Peter wanted to stay here. As the young people would say, "It's a good place to crash." "Lord" said Peter, "this is a beautiful uplifting experience. Let me build three shelters here, one for you, one for Moses and one for Elijah." Perhaps the implication was that he, James and John would share this accommodation!

UNREPEATABILITY OF SOME EXPERIENCE

As I said, how easily we want to capture the experience, to institutionalize, regularize, credalize, and in whatever way we can make it and similar experiences something that we can manage, control and monopolize. Isn't that what the Church did when it saw itself as being the sole dispenser of God's grace on earth? "Come to Christ through our form, our experience, our creed or you cannot come," is what was said. Isn't that what Jesus was rebuking in the disciples when he told them not to worry about the persons who didn't follow and who didn't believe exactly in their manner of following and believing, and when he refused to call down fire from heaven upon them as the disciples wanted Him to do? How often we want to capture the experience, and have it repeated exactly as it was in the first place. The truth of the matter is you can no more totally and accurately repeat a spiritual experience in every detail than you can repeat a sunset. The beauty of the repeated experience may be just as great, the results of it just as significant, but the details are bound to be different and its beauty will be in part because it is not the same as the one of the previous time. We even sing longingly about this, "Where is the blessedness I knew when first I met the Lord? Where is the soul refreshing view, of Jesus and his Word?" The answer is that the blessedness is around us, above us, beneath us, and within us. In that way its presence is refreshed and refreshing.

MOUNTAIN TOP IN A DANCE HALL!

I have never had a repetition of the experience I had on the first Saturday night in October in 1934. I was 14 years of age. It was a Saturday night when our little church, which was really a dance hall commandeered for worship on the weekend, had what was called the "preparatory service." Holy Communion was the next day and it was expected that members of the church would come on Saturday night to "prepare themselves'' for the receiving of the Holy Communion. With two other young people I made my profession of faith. I can remember in detail as if it were last Saturday night, the little platform at the front of the dusty, dingy dancehall ... the minister standing by a little lectern and coming down off the platform to greet two other young people and myself ... my mother sitting at the organ with the coal oil lamp burning on the lamp stand.

When the minister asked the question, "Do you confess Jesus Christ as Saviour and Lord?" and I said, "I do", I knew that something significant and far reaching was happening. I did not know its exact meaning. I had no idea where it would lead me. The thought that it would have led me some places it did would have been almost too frightening to bear. But I knew that somehow it was one of the most important things that had yet happened in my life. Subsequent events may prove it to have been *the* most important. That is why when the report on Christian Initiation was presented to the Halifax General Council in 1980, I felt I would have been less than honest if I did not express my concern that any diminution of the significance of that personal commitment to Jesus Christ as Lord ought not to be taken lightly.

My "confirmation", rightly or wrongly, was a high if not a much higher spiritual experience in my life than my ordination. I make no apology for that. It was, after all, the basic commitment to Jesus Christ as Lord. Everything that has happened since is simply a branch — hopefully a fruit-bearing branch on that true vine. This is not to suggest that my life has always been congruent with the commitment. But then that too is part of the Gospel of redeeming grace.

THE MAJESTY OF GOD EXPERIENCE

Many people can describe a similar or more dramatic experience. You may have had your Mount of Transfiguration experience. I think, for instance, of the story told to me by Dr. Jean Hutchinson. She recounted that her father, who was a very close friend of an Archbishop of the Roman Catholic Church in Halifax during the twenties, had been privy to this personal spiritual experience. This, of course, was in the early part of this century and at a time when Roman Catholics and Protestants did not often speak openly to each other about the meaning of their spiritual life. Mr. Moriarty was a very close friend of the Archbishop and recounts the following story.

The Archbishop and his curate or assistant had been together at a meeting one evening. They returned to their respective quarters for the night. About two o'clock in the morning the younger man awakened and, looking out the window across the courtyard, saw a light burning in the Archbishop's study. Being concerned lest the Prelate was ill, the priest dressed and went across to reassure himself that all was well. He knocked on the study door and a gentle voice said, "Come in." Entering he saw the Archbishop seated in his chair with a book open on his knee. The young man apologized for his intrusion and said, "Your Grace, I am sorry to disturb you but when I awakened and saw a light burning in your room, I came over to make sure that you were alright. I thought perhaps you might be ill." "Oh, it's alright," the elder priest replied, "you see, about midnight I began to meditate on the majesty of God and I became so excited about it I could not get back to sleep."

"I became so excited about it I could not get back to sleep." I ask you when have those of us who preach last been so excited about the majesty of God that we could not sleep? When have those of us who pray last been so excited about the majesty of God that it disturbed our sleep? When have those of us who write last been so excited about the majesty of God that we could not get back to sleep? When have those of us engaged in feverish activity on behalf of the Kingdom last been so excited about the majesty of God that it disturbed our sleep? In other words, we need the mountain top experience but let me hasten to add, WE DARE NOT STAY ON THE MOUNTAIN TOP.

JESUS ONLY

When Peter suggested they build three shelters and abide a while, Jesus would not allow him to do so. He said, "Rise, and have no fear." "And when they lifted up their eyes, they saw no one but Jesus only." This emphasis on the centrality of Jesus, "they saw no one but Jesus only" was an essential ingredient in the story and must be so in relevant faith today. What it says to us is that we should rejoice in the return in the theological thinking of our own church of the understanding of the meaning of "Christology." The question is not only who was Jesus? It is not only who is Jesus? The vital question is what does Jesus mean to me? What does Jesus mean to you?

Recall that six days before this event Jesus had posed that question to the disciples and it was not enough that they replied that some people thought this and other people thought that, the critical question was, "Who do *you* say that I am?" So I am greatly heartened by the fact that confessing our faith and the "saving significance of Jesus in our time" is one of the central themes with which we are called to wrestle in the United Church today. For I still believe that T. R. Glover was near to the truth when he concluded his work on the life of Jesus with the words, "Whatever may be the surprises of history, Jesus will never be surpassed."

INTO THE VALLEY OF DEMONS

But we must press on because there is much more in this story that tells us about God's will for us. The disciples wanted to stay on the mountain top but Jesus refused to allow them to do so. They came down and the first thing they met was extreme human need. A 'demon' had taken possession of one of God's children. The pain and suffering were real both to himself and to those near to him. The disciples were helpless but Jesus effected a transformation in the man's life. He totally altered the situation. He brought peace where there was no peace. He brought wholeness where there had been a fractured personality. He restored reasonableness, sanity and fullness of life for the one who was in distress.

DEMONS — PRESENT DAY MODEL

I saw a demon at work recently in the church in South Africa. It is the easily identifiable demon called *apartheid*. South Africa is the beautiful, rich country that the tourist brochures depict it to be. Untold wealth in gold, diamonds, coal, agriculture, fisheries, all set in the beauty of rolling plains, fertile fields and towering mountains. But South Africa is like a beautiful body with a deadly virus in its bloodstream. That virus is apartheid. The evil doctrine that divides people according to their colour, that in practical application means, for example, that when you reach the age of sixty-five, if you are white, your pension is in the vicinity of $150.00 a month; if you are coloured, your pension is $97.00 a month; and if you are black, your pension is $49.00 a month. When I told that to a white woman in Ontario who was objecting to my criticism of apartheid, her reply was, "Oh well, don't you know that the standard of the blacks over the years has been such that they don't need any more than that!" So much for the logic of those who support apartheid!

But we have the same thing in our own country on a more limited but sometimes not too subtle scale. The Keegstras and Zundels may be found guilty by the courts, and we can thank God for that at the same time as we are depressed by the amount of support accorded in the minds of some in the Canadian public for their racist and anti-semitic views. The Ontario Human Rights Commission reported that people may call for a taxi in Toronto or Kingston and say to the dispatcher, "Be sure and send me a white driver or I will not use your taxi again." The editorial comment in the Globe and Mail about Donald Marshall, the Indian youth who spent eleven years in prison for a crime he did not commit makes a valid observation. "We wonder", it asks, "if he had been white if this would have happened." The subtle racism that has reduced our native population to some kind of third class citizenry; the subtle sexism that has caused many women to feel they are second class citizens; the subtle discrimination so that although there may not be one law for the rich and another for the poor, there is surely one way in which the law is applied to the rich and another way in which it is applied to the poor — these are demons in our midst. Yet some United Church Christians want us to stay on the mountain top praying and never come down in the valley to deal with the demons.

In this regard, I want to share with you the opinion given by one layman, not a member of the United Church, who was present at a retreat I was leading.

A LAYMAN DOCTOR'S WITNESS

This layman expressed the point of view that some people seem to think dealing with these issues is a waste of time or a perversion of the Gospel. "I happen to believe it is the essence of the application of the Gospel," said this doctor, brought up with a fundamentalist approach to the faith but who is now a member of the United Church. He advanced the following three propositions regarding the responsibility of a Christian in today's society:

1. No person or group of persons should exploit any other person or group of persons.
2. The resources of the earth are here for all mankind and not for any individual or nation.
3. Any gifts of special quality of intellect or creativity have been given by God for the benefit of all mankind and we should use them in that direction.

I may add that this doctor is a member of Physicians for Social Responsibility so he puts his energy where his thoughts lead him.

Dr. E. Stanley Jones put the two sides of the coin succinctly when he wrote:

"Works without faith is like a body without a soul. Faith without works is like a soul without a body. One is a corpse — the other a ghost."

We need the mountain top experiences. Without them we are in danger of sterility of thought, barren emotions, expiring hope — in short "burnout". We need also to keep the path from the mountain top of faith to the valley of service well trod. That ways lies wholeness.

Thanks be to God. Amen.

THE CHRIST MIND IN MINISTRY FOR THE EIGHTIES

"This I do know — how again and again the poor thing that has left my lips has been transfigured on its way to the hearer's ears, transfigured into a greater thing and into a quickening thing. And when I am told of these things, I have to say quietly to myself: I believe in the Holy Ghost ..... God is somehow, somewhere in this business, that makes it tolerable and sane and rational."

Dr. Richard Roberts
Former Moderator, The United Church of Canada
(The Gospel at Corinth — p.35)

Professor John Knox, formerly professor at Union Theological Seminary, writes of his father Absalom Knox. "..... when I think of him as preacher ..... I think of the seriousness with which he took his preaching and the absolute honesty with which he did it, the long and careful work he devoted to preparing for it, the biblical quality of it, its solidity and wholeness, the way it answered to the life of the church, the way it spoke to the heart." (The Integrity of Preaching)

THE CHRIST MIND IN MINISTRY FOR THE EIGHTIES
(A sermon preached at the time of the Ordination of Ministers)

Text: "Let this mind be in you which was also in Christ Jesus."

Phil: 2:5

INTRODUCTION

A student about to go out to preach for the weekend in my Alma Mater of Pine Hill Divinity Hall, asked one of his theological professors what he should preach about. The professor replied, "You should preach about God and you should preach about twenty minutes." I wish to preach about the Christ Mind in Ministry for the Eighties, and about twenty minutes. My text, you have probably guessed, is to be found in St. Paul's letter to the Church of Philippi, Chapter 2 and verse 5, "Let this mind be in you which was also in Christ Jesus."

TRADITIONAL AND CONTEMPORARY

These words have about them a note of grandeur and a ring of truth that sets them apart. They are a sort of "hallelujah chorus" coming in the midst of an already majestic composition. They pick up the nuances of classical theology, "who though he was in the form of God"; or the affirmation of the "incarnational" nature of our faith — "the cosmic Christ" referred to in Colossians, as well as the "word become flesh" as put forth by St. John. They reflect that time in history when

God took the great warm mother/father arms of love and wrapped them around the world and said, "I love you." They also connote the theology of "identification" or "liberation." "He emptied himself and took the form of a servant," and at the same time these words lift up the Cross and hold out to us a Christo-centric faith. Sisters and brothers you won't take the heart out of it by allowing something or someone else to take the place that belongs to Christ as the Revealer of the love of God — will you? And you won't lop off the arms and legs of this faith by reducing it to prayer, piety and pie in the sky, bye and bye — please don't do that!

One of the great signs of hope for the church in our time is the manner in which in the church, the arts, music, literature, drama, theology and action are centering on what it means to be faithful to the person of Jesus Christ — "the life of the world," to use the World Council of Churches theme. It is not only who Jesus was but who Jesus is or can be to us today. This is one of the major signs of hope in our time.

A THEOLOGICAL ADVENTURE

You are coming into the ministry at a time when our church is engaged in a quiet but what could be a revolutionary theological adventure. We are concentrating on the theme, "Confessing our Faith — The Saving Significance of Jesus for Our Time" and the meaning of the acknowledgement of God in history and in our midst. This can be one of the most exhilarating, mind stretching, soul stirring and life engaging things to happen in our church for decades. Or it can be a sentimental, spiritual binge and an unmitigated disaster if we become an introverted, inward looking, clubby, chummy, groovy group with congregational and denominational isolationism. The saving significance of Jesus, the lifting up of the person of Christ with emphasis on the relevance of Jesus for our time and God in our midst cannot but be good news if it is carried out in faithfulness to the Gospel.

AN UNCERTAIN SOUND

Many people have been troubled by what seems at times to be the ambivalence, the equivocal, the hesitant and uncertain sound of the gospel trumpet in the last couple of decades. During that time we have been picking ourselves up from the debris of the fall-out from the God is dead theology and liberalism gone to seed. I speak here of "liberalism gone to seed" not just liberalism. There is no need for liberalism in its best sense to be shallow or trite. When Karl Barth was asked if he was a liberal in matters theological he replied that he would have to define what he meant by liberal and the answer would be "yes." He went on to say "by liberal I mean to be open and responsible." We cannot substitute a social gospel for a personal gospel or a personal gospel for a social gospel without destroying the gospel which has personal and social dimensions. Personally, as I have indicated elsewhere, I am an unashamed evangelical and an unrepentant social activist. But it is true we have sometimes given evidence of not being too sure of our gospel or of its meaning for us. The result has been a kind of failure of spiritual nerve or a lack of moral courage. The way back or better, the way forward, is not going to be without its hazards and its pain. No journey ever is — especially when it is a faith journey. You, as new members of the Order of Ministry, will have to be transmitters of the light which will guide us through the darkness, a staff on which to lean when the way is rough and steep, and a hope that beckons us on in the midst of sullen despair. Such light and support may better be yours if you take a closer look at these words, "Let this mind be in you which was also in Christ Jesus." Read these words over and over again. Do with them as you ought to do with any scripture before you preach from it. Marinate your minds in the scriptures. Let your mind soak up the flavour, the spice, the effervescence, and sparkling, tingling wine of the scriptures and the spirit in which the scriptures were written and ought to be read — and indeed lived!

NOT AN EASY TIME FOR YOU

On March 31st, 1943, I was ordained to the ministry of the Church at St. John's United Church in Halifax. A minister who was retiring that year said to me: "Clarke, I wish I was where you are; but I can tell you, I think it is going to be harder for you in the next forty years than it was for me in the last forty." He was not referring to physical hardships I am sure, because when he started out in the ministry in 1903, the going was mighty tough in a physical sense. What he meant was that there would be more difficult issues to face, more traumatic decisions to be made and challenges to be met. So I can say to you — "Its going to be tougher for you than it was for me." When we heard at the World Council of Churches that there "were more martyrs in this century than any century since the time of Jesus Christ" we realized what those words meant in many parts of our world and what they may mean for Christians in any part of the world in the years ahead.

But two questions present themselves, the answers to which instruct us well on this occasion.

1. What does it mean to have the mind which was in Christ?
2. How do we attain this state of mind?

WHAT DOES IT MEAN?

We hear tell of people who are what we call "look-a-likes". I recently met three people all of whom told me that they were mistaken for me on a certain occasion — I cannot understand why they would broadcast that fact! There are also people whom we might call "think-a-likes". It means their approach to issues, their sense of values, their appreciation of life, their response to its demands and opportunities are similar. They are on the same wave length. They quickly pick up each other's "vibes." Paul is saying here "Be on the same wave length with Christ — be a think-a-like with him."

CLOTHED IN THE MIND OF CHRIST

Roger Roy, the witty and sophisticated director of the play, "Let My People Come" — a play which I have never seen — was being interviewed. I heard him offer a defence against the critique that in one scene of the play the actors and actresses appear on the stage clothed only in a pair of ballet slippers! He gave the rationale in these delicately crafted words, "They wear their nudity as a costume." My response when asked for a comment was, "When they go on the road I hope they don't lose their luggage!" Wear the mind of Christ, not as a costume for play acting, but as street clothing for the daily walk of life. "Be clothed with the mind which was also in Christ Jesus."

JESUS STOOD TALL BY STOOPING LOW.

Let us take a vingette — a little slice of life — from Jesus' experience and see how this works.

Jesus is in the Upper Room in Jerusalem. The shadow of the cross lengthened on his trail. He has an overpowering sense of mission and of destiny. St. John puts it this way, "Jesus knowing that he came from God and went to God, took a towel and girded himself and washed the disciples' feet." Note the unique melding here of majesty and humility — even of divinity and humanity. "Jesus knowing that he came from God and was going to god" did what? Well, what would the average mortal do? What did the gods of mythology do? They sought power and position. They made incredible demands on themselves, on others and on the fates. They wanted to be number one. When Ronald Reagan suggested that America be number one again he called upon America to "stand tall amongst the nations of the world". To him standing tall meant to have power and be feared. It meant to be able to order other nations as to what kind of government they should have and, if they did not obey, to bring economic, military and other pressures to bear upon them to force them into conformity. In Jesus case to be number one meant not to stand tall but to stoop down. "He took a towel, girded himself, wrapped it around him, and kneeling down began to wash the disciples' feet." He did the task long considered the most menial task for the most menial slave.

When the Christian ministry deserts the servant role, it loses its integrity. However eloquent your preaching may be; however many appendages to your name indicating your academic achievements; however bedecked you are with honorific titles; however rewarded by ecclesiastical appointments or advancements; you will never have a higher calling than this, "He took a towel and girded himself."

LIBERATION OF THE MARGINALIZED

I receive letters from people who tell me they will leave the United Church if we go against the policies of the Department of National Defence, and the national budget; if we support collective bargaining, if we ordain homosexuals. I have yet to receive a letter from anyone who says that he/she is going to leave the United Church because we don't take seriously enough the admonition of Jesus, "I have set you an example that as I have loved you so you ought to love one another." No one has ever said they will leave the United Church because we don't do enough on behalf of the poor or against war. Women, blacks, coloured, indigenous peoples, the unemployed and the marginalized of every sort invite us to declare how we interpret the gospel and what obedience to the gospel means. Their fondest dreams and deepest aspirations are often summed up in the word "liberation". The name of the first liberation theologian was Moses. Liberation is not a word someone coined in the seclusion of the theological study or one which was invented by those who toy with metaphysical concepts, neither does it come from petty compromise with communism. This word was forged out of the experience of God's people faced with oppression and abuse. They know what liberation is because they know what lack of it means.

THREE VIGNETTES — LITTLE SLICES OF LIFE

"Cheryl", the coloured woman who with her black three year old nephew took my wife and me to the beach at Capetown in South Africa and had to try four different roads before she found a beach that was not "for whites only" does not need to attend a workshop on the subject of liberation to decide what it means. She knows what liberation means from her experience of what lack of it implies.

Beyers Naude, a white man who left the white Dutch Reformed Church of South Africa to join the Dutch Reformed Mission Church because of apartheid was under banning orders when we were in South Africa. He made this pertinent observation: "I have been banned for five years but a black person is banned from the day of birth to the day of death."

Rosa Parks sat stoically at the front of a bus in Birmingham, Alabama when the driver pointing to the back said, "Niggers to the back of the bus" and she replied, "My feets gettin' mighty tired of this sort of thing and God's gettin' mighty tired of it too — and I am going to stay where I am." She was expressing her concept of liberation based on the servant image and she started something which shook the American establishment from that seat at the front of the bus to the seats of justice in Washington. As someone put it, "When Rosa Parks sat down the whole world stood up."

This word "liberation" is no crypto communist word that has somehow crept into the vocabulary of the Christian. This is a word that was front and centre from "the slave pens of the delta" to the "strange man on his Cross" who "emptied his life" that we might be "free at last, free at last, thank the Lord God Almighty, free at last!"

GRASPING THAT CHRIST MIND —
OR BEING GRASPED BY IT

We speak now of how this "mind which was in Christ Jesus" may become our mind as well. This implies — in fact requires what in the New Testament is called "metanoia". This is the "about face". This is the U- turn in our lives. Such a transformation is directly related to how one thinks of and responds to Jesus. Wherever your ministry leads you it will never surpass the need to present Christ to men and women and youth as their Saviour and Lord, and to society as its liberator. If your ministry is led by the Spirit of Christ, while you may plan your ministry in a general sort of way, you will not determine it fully but be ever sensitive to that tap on the shoulder of your mind when the Spirit calls and you respond.

Some time ago, with about thirty members of the United Church of Canada, I shared the premises of the Five Oaks Centre with about fifty men and women from Alcoholics Anonymous. We were together for meals, for bed time snacks and on Sunday morning for Holy Communion. It was a rich mix of people who realized before long how much they had in common. There was the young church woman in our group. She was so poised, apparently so self confident, so sure of the direction in which her life was going and yet seeking meaning for her life by probing the mind that is in Christ. Then there was the young man in Alcoholics Anonymous who knew he had to live a day at a time, who knew from experience he was "one drink from a drunk" and that he had to pray for deliverance every hour. I asked myself what do these two people have in common? It soon became obvious. They both acknowledged their finiteness. They both acknowledged their need of God. They both believed they were here for a purpose. They both knew they needed the support and shared strength of each other, of persons like themselves and of the living presence of Christ as each understood it.

NOT JUST PETER — BUT JUDAS TOO. . .

We need to recall that in that Upper Room Jesus washed the feet of Judas as well as of Peter, of the activist James as well as the spiritually minded John. When you strip us of our position, our outward power — be it achieved, inherited or appointed — our wealth or lack of it, the difference between the men who ate lunch at a church mission this morning, or the "bag lady" in a downtown street and ourselves, is not all that significant. I think that is why Jesus said that in the final analysis only God is to judge between us. In discharging the task assigned to me by the General Council in 1982 in relation to Archambault Prison and the subsequent events following the riot there on July 25th of that year, I spent six hours locked in a small cell talking with five prisoners all of whom are in for murder and for twenty-five years imprisonment without eligibility for parole. When I came home to write the report requested at that time by the Solicitor General, Honourable Robert Kaplan, I wrote in red ink across my personal copy of my report about these men: "There but for the Grace of God goes Clarke MacDonald."

The mind that was in Christ is bigger than our sometimes petty ideologies. There is a fundamentalism of the left and a fundamentalism of the right that we must avoid with all our heart, soul, mind and strength if we are to live the fullness of the Gospel message. "Let this mind be in you which was also in Christ Jesus." It was a mind that was bigger, grander and more inclusive than anything our small minds can possibly comprehend. Did you read the somewhat obscure note in the account of a crash about two years ago of a Boeing 747 airplane in the Potomac River? The story was entitled "The Man in the Water". He was referred to in the story as "the balding man with the wild mustache." Survivors were floating about in the chilly water clinging to bits and pieces of the craft. Five people were in a cluster of floating debris. A helicopter descended, lowering a grappling hook which the balding man with the wild mustache caught and immediately passed to another person floating in the water. Two, three, four times the helicopter came and went, descended, lowered the grappling hook and each time the balding man with the wild mustache caught it and passed it to someone else. When the craft returned the fifth time to pick up "the man in the water" — he was gone. No one knew anything about him other than that he was "the man in the water — the balding man with the wild mustache."

Was he Christian, Jew, Muslim, Buddhist or atheist? We don't know. Was he capitalist or communist? Was he democrat or republican? We don't know. Was he heterosexual or homosexual? I don't know. But I do believe in that moment that a voice from somewhere said, "inasmuch as you passed the grappling hook to one of these, you passed it to me." If that isn't so, then I should go home and take the scissors and deliberately cut the twenty-fifth chapter of St. Matthew out of my New Testament because it does not mean what it says and it does not make sense.

NO SHORT CUTS — PLEASE!

It is much easier to live with the implication of saying "Jesus Christ is Saviour" than to live with the implication of saying, "Jesus Christ is Lord." To confess the first means a burden is lifted. To affirm the second means a responsibility is undertaken. I never lie awake at night wondering if I am saved. That was settled when I acknowledged Jesus Christ as Saviour. I don't spend five minutes or five seconds worrying about going to heaven or hell — "I know whom I have believed." But I do anguish over what it means to say "Jesus Christ is Lord." What it means for you to confess this in your ministry and how you will exercise it will determine the style of ministry which you will bring to the latter half of this decade and to the last decade of this century. We are called to obedience and faithfulness not to getting by in sloth and slackness. You will be a successful minister if you never forget the towel and the basin. Go forth then in the power of the living God. Go forth knowing that you do not walk alone and maintain within you that mind which was in Christ Jesus. Perhaps the words of the hymn that has become a favourite of many will assist you in your launching tonight.

> I feel the winds of God today;
> today my sail I lift,
> though heavy oft with drenching spray
> and torn with many a rift;
> if hope but light the water's crest,
> and Christ my bark will use,
> I'll seek the seas at his behest,
> and brave another cruise.

God bless you and use you to the glory of God in the service of Christ and to the joy of the Holy Spirit. Amen.

THE CHURCH
UNDER THE CROSS

"Batter my heart, three
personed God; for You
As yet but knock, breathe,
shine, and seek to mend;
That I may rise and stand,
o'er throw me, and bend
Your force, to break, blow,
burn, and make me new."

John Donne — Holy Sonnets

"When I was minister at Saint Luke's Church in downtown
Toronto the cross was stolen from the Communion Table. The
caretaker and I from past experience in other thefts, had an
idea where it would be found. It was located in a pawn shop
on the Yonge Street Strip. When we retrieved it and placed it
back on the Communion Table I could not help but reflect —
'Have we done the right thing?' Should the cross be safely
ensconced on the Communion Table reflecting the beautiful
colours of sunlight filtered through stained glass windows — or
should it be on 'the Strip' — where the races of the world go
by, where obscenities are uttered, where Jesus is profaned by
people who profess to love him, as well as those who hate him
— even a few doors from the place where the 'shoeshine boy'
Emmanuel Jacques was murdered?"

THE CHURCH UNDER THE CROSS

Text: "If anyone wants to be my disciple he/she
must forget self, carry the Cross and follow
me."

St. Matthew 16:24

On a Good Friday morning, Muriel and I went to worship at Bloor Street United Church in Toronto. This service was a moving experience with appropriate music, scriptures and prayers. Dr. Lois Wilson preached the sermon. She was in an unusually subdued mood. I say unusual because she is known for the energetic and enthusiastic way in which she ordinarily speaks. But she was no less passionate and was deeply concerned. She was recounting in part her visits to Central America and South Korea. She was subdued because she was speaking of the pain of the people, the suffering of the church. She had learned of priests murdered, nuns raped, ministers and students and lay people who were the target of torture and oppression. She had joined the "May Day Mothers" in the City Square in Argentina. They were protesting the disappearance of fathers, brothers, sons and husbands into the darkness of the night never to be heard of again. She linked all of this to the Cross of our Lord Jesus Christ. She conveyed the feeling that Calvary was right there is our midst. The body of Christ was being crucified afresh in our world.

From this service, we, along with many other congregations, went to the street on which Litton Industries is located. We were joined by people, both Roman Catholic and

Protestant, who had been worshipping at other churches. We were protesting the twenty-seven million dollars of our tax money which goes to help this industry produce the guidance system for the cruise missile. This is a nuclear weapon of mega-death proportions launched from B-52 bombers. This protest was carried out in a very peaceful manner with prayers and readings and meditations along the way.

ELECTRONIC EVANGELIST

About mid-afternoon we returned home and I switched on the television to find Jim Bakker, one of the "electronic evangelists" and his wife Tammy "doing their thing" before the TV cameras. In his affable manner Jim Bakker was telling about a personal experience of pain and frustration he had had the previous night. He told the story well, building up the suspense until you wondered what it could be. Had he spent the night counselling some "sorely charged mind"? Had he been called out from his home, as many of us have after midnight, to talk with an alcoholic or to visit someone who was dying? What could be the nature of the trauma that caused such agony? Finally, he came to the point. It was none of these. At 2.30 that morning he had been awakened by plaintiff cries from their pet cat. The animal had been trapped on the roof by the neighbour's dog. He subdued the canine intruder and with flashlight and ladder rescued the feline pet. This came over on Good Friday morning as being a cross-bearing experience! I thought back to Lois' sermon — to the Good Friday morning service at Bloor Street — to the walk to and the prayers and meditations at Litton, including our prayers for the survival of the planet. With these reflections the only appropriate thing to do was to turn Jim Bakker off!*

How we tend to trivialize the Cross. Everything from the cat trapped on the roof by the neighbour's dog, to a toothache, to a rundown car battery, to a leaky faucet becomes — "our cross to bear".

---

* Since this was written we've learned of the illness of Tammy Bakker and the trauma through which they are both going. "Love is never glad when others go wrong," so we pray for their wholeness and health.

JOSE OF MORIJA

Let me give you another picture in words. It was at the theological college in Morija, Lusotho, that I met Jose. When Rev. George Halliday, the principal of the college introduced us, I thought probably Jose had been a victim of polio or a severe attack of arthritis. His hands looked as though the fingers had been fused together and he walked with an uncertain gait. As we talked for two hours he told me his story. Caught as he was in the mish-mash of political intrigue that the application of the apartheid doctrine forces upon Southern Africa including this unhappy, landlocked country, President Jonathon's forces had rounded up certain people among whom was Jose. In an attempt to extract information from him which he did not possess, he was tortured. In a quiet, almost detached manner, and without the slightest trace of revenge or desire to get even, he described what happened.

THE TORTURE

His hands were tied loosely behind his back and then a twister — the kind a trucker uses to bind a load of logs onto his truck — was inserted in the slack rope and turned by two men until the bones, muscles and tendons were cracked, crunched and torn. While this was going on another man was attacking his ankle bones with a hammer! "I was lucky", he said quietly, "some people died under that kind of treatment." I could only think that under such circumstances I might pray earnestly that I would die. To end the account on a more happy note, let me tell you that when I was Moderator and visited the Newfoundland and Labrador Conference, I told about Jose at practically every service. The people donated $1,300, which was sent to Morija Theological College to help Jose get surgical treatment on his hands and feet. He can walk and write now. A Lutheran Church in Germany at the same time sent money to purchase a donkey for him so he can ride up into the hills and hinterland of Lusotho. This very day he is likely there with his donkey and in his gentle and persuasive way sharing the good news of the word of life in his loving and convincing manner — that's what I call Cross bearing. Like Jesus before Pilate, Jose could have avoided this. He could have compromised. Jesus could have sold his integrity for less than Judas charged for his body — thirty pieces of silver. Jose could have sold his people for a pittance. But he chose to fulfil the message of our text. "Do you want to be my disciple?", said Jesus. "I do", said Jose. "Then forget yourself", said Jesus. "I will", said Jose. "Then carry your Cross and follow me", said Jesus. "I will", said Jose — and he did.

THE CHOICE WAS JESUS' OWN

Because he was weakened by trial and torture Jesus could not carry his Cross, and Simeon the Syrenian was pressed into service. But the choice to go the way of the Cross was Jesus' own. It was a decision forged in the heat of temptation in the wilderness, tempered to hardened steel in encounter and confrontation in the marketplace, brought to white heat in the Garden of Gethsemane and confirmed on the Cross when he cried out, "Father into your hands I commit my spirit."

PUT IT IN CONTEMPORARY TERMS

Now how do we translate this into meaningful terms for us today? Let me try to do so briefly under three headings.
1. The first has already been alluded to. We each must accept his/her own cross. No one else can do it for us.
2. The Cross reveals the vulnerability of God — even God's weakness it would seem.
3. The Cross, and its central message for our time, as for all time, is the supreme revelation of God's love for all humankind throughout the world. It is that moment when, as St. John said, "grace was heaped upon grace."

1. IT MUST BE A MATTER OF CHOICE

Some people confuse what they cannot avoid and are forced to bear with cross bearing. This is wrong. If I found out tomorrow that I had a terminal illness, I hope I would not say, "This is my Cross, I must bear it." If I found out, as too many are, that my marriage was on the rocks, I hope I would not say, "This is my Cross, I must bear it." If I found out that I was betrayed by friends and Church and all had deserted me, I hope I would not say, "This is my Cross, I must bear it." Wherein, then, in these situations do I find the Cross and wherein am I able to say, "I take up my Cross to follow Christ."? I find the Cross not in the inescapable event itself but in my response to it. If, in the event of the doctor's verdict about a terminal illness, I were to denounce God (as I may well at first do) that is not accepting my Cross. The illness then is not my Cross. In that I have no choice. I am accepting my Cross when I say, "Now, God, that this has hit me, what can you and I do together to make it worthwhile? How can it redound to your glory so that I can say with Job, 'though he smite me, yet will I trust him.' "

Let me illustrate this from the experience of a cross-bearing brother. Professor Robert (Bob) Osborne, a minister and professor of religion at Carleton University, retired in June, 1985. That fall he and his wife, Beverley, moved to Victoria, B.C. Soon after their arrival Bob became ill and was diagnosed as having inoperable cancer. He died February 2nd of the following year. On January 28th, five days before his death, he wrote a letter from which I quote: "Many of you ask about my illness. I have inoperable cancer .... most days I am able to get up and sit in the family room .... Beverley and I are able to spend many happy hours together .... we enjoy each day, each hour as it comes. My only regret now is that I will soon have to leave Beverley alone. My faith in the gospel has been a constant support and I can echo Dr. Martin Niemoller's words, 'in the old days I carried the gospel. Now that gospel carries me.' Thank you for keeping us in your thoughts and prayers. I am getting tired so I will close now. I look forward to meeting you all again on a brighter shore. 'For I am sure that neither death, nor life, nor angels, nor principalities, nor things present, nor things to come, nor powers, nor height, nor depth, nor anything else in all creation, will be able to separate us from the love of God in our Lord Jesus Christ.' (Romans 8: 33-39)

Love to all of you. Bob."

This is what I mean by choice and that is what I mean by cross-bearing. Bob chose to turn a tragedy into a triumph. He took a disappointment and turned it into God's appointment. He even transformed death into life. He took up the Cross, not grudgingly but with a glad heart and celebrated the fact that, "nothing can separate us from the love of God in Jesus Christ our Lord." In so doing he has left all who hear his words in his debt and set for us an example. To do this is a matter of choice. We must choose. Clarke MacDonald cannot bear someone else's Cross and no one else can bear his.

2. THE VULNERABILITY OF GOD

If we believe in the Omnipotence of God, the possibilities of what God could have done at creation are limitless. God could have created us as robots, as puppets dancing on the end of some divine string. The decision to leave us free to choose good or evil left God wide open to our attacks. To that degree God is responsible for our sin. To that degree God is responsible for the Cross. To that degree God is responsible for the holocaust. To that degree God is responsible for the possibility of the destruction of all things on the planet Earth.

Tough Theology

This is tough stuff, theologically speaking. But you don't want theological pap, do you? Stay with me (or better stay with God) and see if we can't work our way through this. Stay with God to whom "a thousand years is but as one day". I am no literalist but for a moment think of it in those terms and then you will realize it was only three days ago that Moses crossed the Red Sea! Two and one-half days ago Isaiah, Jeremiah and Amos thundered forth their prophecies. Two days ago Jesus was born in Bethlehem and the Crucifixion and Resurrection happened within the last forty-eight hours. So you see God is and will work out the purposes God had in creation. We are fools if we think that because we have the power to destroy creation we can totally thwart God's plan. The dispensationalists — the people whose fixation is Armageddon — are in danger of doing just that. President Ronald Reagan used the word 'Armageddon' eight times during his recent campaign speeches for the presidency. It is frightening to think that a man with such a theological notion is the most powerful man on the planet Earth today. It is frightening because if such a man were ever to press the button that would unleash the forces of megadeath in such proportions as to bring nuclear winter to the entire planet for at least six months, he would rationalize it by saying he was an instrument in the hand of God. Instrument in the hand of God — rubbish! He would simply be taking things into his own hands, breaking the first commandment and perhaps committing the unforgivable sin. But you see this is the window of vulnerability which God has left open toward the people who think in these perverse theological terms and it should only strengthen our resolve to press forward in peace work for the future of our children and of the planet Earth.

God Risked Everything

As people of the Incarnation and the Resurrection we must not despair at this point. I find the experience recounted by a Jewish youth in the Auschwitz prison camp to be of profound assurance here.

Elie Wiesel tells of a day the S.S. commander sentenced a fourteen year old youth to death on the gallows along with two adults. In the camp they called the boy ''a child with a refined and beautiful face'', the ''sad eyed angel''. He writes:

> ''One day when we came back from work, we saw three gallows. Three victims in chains — and one of them, the little servant, the sad-eyed angel. To hang a young boy in front of thousands of spectators was no light matter. The head of the camp read the verdict. All eyes were on the child. He was lividly pale, almost calm, biting his lips. The three victims mounted together onto the chairs. The three necks were placed at the same moment within the nooses.
> 'Long live liberty,' cried the two adults.
> But the child was silent.
> 'Where is God? Where is He?' someone behind me asked.
> At a sign from the head of the camp, the three chairs tipped over.
> Total silence throughout the camp.
> Then the march past began. The two adults were no longer alive. Their tongues hung swollen, blue-

tinged. But the third rope was still moving; being so light, the child was still alive...
For more than half an hour he stayed there, struggling between life and death, dying in slow agony under our eyes. And we had to look him full in the face. He was still alive when I passed in front of him. His tongue was still red, his eyes were not yet glazed.
Behind me, I heard the same man asking:
'Where is God now?'
And I heard a voice within me answer him:
'Where is He? Here He is — He is hanging here on this gallows.' "

Yes — a thousand times yes!

With the child — on the gallows — as God was with the Only Begotten on the Cross. "Father into your hands I yield my spirit." God took the risk of being vulnerable by putting all God had on the table believing that love would win at the last. Is the Church prepared to run that risk today?

3. THE CENTRAL MESSAGE IS GOD SAYING "I LOVE YOU."

Dr. Richard Roberts, a native of Wales, one time minister in Toronto and a past Moderator of the United Church, tells a story out of his youth as a student minister in his homeland. He had been called home because of the serious illness of his father. He was sitting by his father's bed where the old man seemed to lie in a state of unconsciousness. Suddenly his father stirred and waved his hand toward the table and said simply, "the book". Richard Roberts knew what he meant so he picked up the Bible. He also knew the passage he wanted to have read. He opened it at the passage quoted by Professor Robert Osborne as I mentioned earlier in this sermon. In the eighth chapter of Romans, "nothing can separate us from the love of God in Jesus Christ our Lord." After he had read the passage Richard Roberts looked at his father and said, "Does it hold now father? Does it hold now?" The old man's eyelids flickered and a gentle smile of confidence crossed his face as he whispered back to his son, "Yes, son, it holds now. It holds now."

And so it does still hold. It holds for Bishop Tutu as he combats the principalities and powers in his own land. It holds for the May Day Mothers in Argentina and the students jailed in South Korea. It holds for the people who go to worship and the ministers who preach and the priests who celebrate the Eucharist with deep devotion and high hope in countries where the secret police are dogging their footsteps.

Because, you see, a love like that in Jesus Christ is unbeatable. Our pale imitations of it often falter and we ourselves feel defeated. When the worst the world had to offer was vented — spewed, if you will — on Jesus, the best in Jesus — the best of love, of grace, of courage and of hope burst forth from his being (like the blood and water from the spear point in his side) and flowed out toward his tormentors and to all people, world without end. That love, grace and courage have been flooding the world ever since that time. The Church as the Body of Christ is both the receiver and the servant of that love. Pray to God we will be equal to the task.

Thanks be to God. Amen.

AMAZING GRACE

(To the tune of Amazing Grace)
Amazing Grace that God who made
Life vast and full and free,
Such grace, and love and truth should share
with folk like you and me.

Help us, O Lord, this grace to show
in glance and speech and deed,
So humankind throughout the world
your love and truth may heed.

God, may this grace your people save
From all their fear and greed,
And all your children live at peace
In every land and creed.

Grant us the grace of faith and trust
Your mission to fulfil,
So that in life beyond this life,
We'll know your perfect will.

Clarke MacDonald (1985)

AMAZING GRACE

Text: Out of his full store we have all received grace upon grace, for while the law was given by Moses, grace and truth came through Jesus Christ.

St. John 1:16-17

A WOMEN'S PRISON

The dark, grey stone walls of a New York State women's prison presented a formidable picture to the fifteen members of the Church and Society Department of the National Council of Churches and myself as we pulled up before the security gate. Pictures were taken, fingerprints secured, and passes were issued as we entered through a clanging door. We were searched by electronic surveillance eyes and finally ushered into the maximum security section of the prison. The women wore drab, coarse uniforms, orders were barked at the prisoners by domineering attendants. Smiles were seldom seen and tension charged the air. The prisoners had to be in their cells at 7 p.m. when the doors were closed from a centrally located electronic switch which opened them again at 7 a.m.

From this place we were taken to the "honour section". Here the women who had achieved a certain number of points were free to go and come from their cells at will. There was a television in the main assembly area and a kitchenette where they could make some coffee. The atmosphere was less formal and rigid. The women were given material to make their own clothes. As we passed by a group of women making coffee, I heard one say to another, "I hope you are going to show your paintings to these visitors." A young woman, neatly attired and soft spoken said, "Perhaps I will." "Are you an artist?" I asked, "if so, I would like to see your paintings." She took me down the corridor to her cell. It was about 10' x 6' with very high walls. The entire wall area was covered with seascapes, landscapes and pastoral scenes with cows and horses grazing in the meadows. In the very centre were the pictures of two beautiful little children. "Are those your children?" I asked. She told me they were and that they came to visit her once a month. "Do you mind if I ask why you are here and for how long?" I enquired. She spoke quietly and without acrimony. "I am here", she replied, "for a very foolish reason. I was sharing my apartment with a man. I thought he was honest. He seemed to care very much about me and my children. One day the police came and raided the apartment seizing a sizeable quantity of drugs. I knew nothing at all about this. He had apparently been tipped off about the raid so he skipped out. Having no one to corroborate my story I had to take the rap. I got fifteen years to life!"

We talked further about her children, her hopes for them and her paintings. We did not speak again about her own future. Later the directress of the prison referring to her and one or two others said, "There is no way they should still be here but the law must take its course." In a dinner speech that night the Deputy Governor of Prisons for the State of New York told us the same thing. All applications for parole had been turned down and as usual no reasons were given. It looks as if she will have to complete her sentence. The law as law cannot forgive. If it were to do that it would cease to be law. Only grace can forgive. "The law was given by Moses but grace and truth came by Jesus Christ."

Each of us has daily acquaintance with law, both the laws of nature and of society. If it were not for the law of gravitation we could not get out of bed to begin our day's work — neither could we stay in bed! We acquiesce daily in these laws about breathing, resting, eating, sleeping, exercising. Nature, like duty, is a "stern daughter of the voice of God" and we know that to stay alive her laws must be honoured. We are free to transgress but the result will be pain and regret. In our human society the case is the same. As you drove to this service you obeyed a dozen laws imposed by society, such as speed limits, traffic lights, turning signals and many others.

OUR KNOWLEDGE OF GRACE

Is our knowledge of and experience of grace as intimate as this? It ought to be. It is by the grace of providence — that is the providing power of God — that we are here. Life itself is a sheer act of grace and so is its being sustained. Think of the many times you might have been done in by illness, anxiety, mental fatigue and you will say, "but for the grace of God that would have been the end." My mother confided in me one time in a moment of intimacy that I was very frail as an infant and weighed less when I was six months old than I did when I was born. I told that to a Cape Bretoner and he said, "Well, imagine that now — and did you live?" The answer is, "Yes — but only by the grace of God." More than that — our very reason for being and for being here is a matter of grace. You don't own this church the way you own your cars or your shoes. All that we do here and the resources to do it are a sheer gift of grace. The music, the poetry, the bible, the liturgy — but again more than that — the spirit of our forebears who caught the vision and saw the potential, the labours of love and gifts of love and prayers which have sustained what goes into the meaning of what we do here — all these are the result of grace heaped upon grace. "The law was given by Moses but grace and truth came by Jesus Christ."

FAITH AS A GIFT OF GRACE

And what shall we say of faith itself? Our very finding of God is an act of His grace not just of our wills. We didn't say, "Set to now we'll find a God like Jesus." God himself set to and said, "I'll show them what I am like, I will show them that I am like Jesus because Jesus and I are one." Grace is the supreme act of God in bridging the gap which exists between ourselves and Himself. We certainly did not earn the right to this faith. If anyone here thinks he/she earned that right, then let him/her stand forth and declare it. Let us call a news conference and tell the world about it because no one else in 2,000 years has successfully made that claim.

My faith and my being here to celebrate it are the result of many factors, most of which were beyond my control and are the product of grace. A host of people, some of whom I have known, many of whom I have never seen, some of whom I have never heard of — have handed on to me and to you the faith of which we have read and sung and about which we prayed and of which I now preach. This is the Lord's doing — it is grace heaped upon grace.

LAW IN CONTRAST TO GRACE

But let us look again at law in contrast to grace. The two are not in irreconcilable conflict. They are complementary, needing each other, supporting each other and together making for fulness and meaning which is brought to the perfect amalgam in the life of Jesus of Nazareth. To understand what St. John was driving at when he said, "the law was given by Moses, but grace and truth came by Jesus Christ", we need to understand how the Jew felt about the law.

(a) To the Jew, and this would include John, Jesus, Peter and the others, the law was not an inert mass of codes and rules. It was a vital living thing. It had daily meaning related to food, dress, treatment of slaves, health, foreigners, sexuality and much more. Its foundation was in a covenant between God and Israel. God acted on behalf of Israel. He demanded a response and gave the Jews a promise that, if they responded positively, they would become a great people.

(b) It was also law applied in community. It was not just between the individual and God but between the individual and God and his neighbour. They were part of a liberated community — a committed community. The Bible had rough language to describe those who failed to be true to the commitment. It said they were "whores"!

(c) This law was summarized in the Ten Commandments. They were not a pat on the head. It was not God saying, "You be nice Israel and I will do nice things for you." The Jews were called to obedience

65

without qualification. "Obey me Yahweh, and you will live, fail to do so and you will die."

This law as expressed in the Torah was an awesome thing. It is no wonder there was smoke, thunder and lightning when God delivered the law to Moses and Moses to the people. Even if Cecile B. DeMille and Charlton Heston made more of that than God did! It was, nevertheless, almost a fearsome experience. I recall one time I was preaching in a Jewish synagogue. At a certain point in the service two elders of the congregation came to the front of the synagogue. They opened the doors to the Ark of the Covenant where the Torah — law — was kept. When they did so there was a blast of trumpets and the people shouted in exaltation. That was the high point of worship for them just as the high point of worship for us is when the officiating minister lifts the bread and the cup and says, "The Body of Christ broken for you," "The Blood of Christ shed for you." That was to them their moment of liberation as the Cross was the moment of our liberation from sin. To the Israelite, then as well as to John and Jesus, all of whom were brought up in this very strong tradition, the law was a living thing. It was meant to be obeyed in community. It was also a consuming fire.

GRACE AS AN OVER PLUS

"But grace came by Jesus Christ." Obviously the law was not enough, something more was needed for the completion of a meaningful relationship between God and his people. That "something more" was provided in Jesus Christ. Revert again to the verse before this one and sense John's complete amazement at what the situation is: "Out of his full store we have all received grace heaped upon grace."

John Oman, a theologian of the first half of this century, who wrote a classic entitled simply "Grace" referred to the grace of God as "the love of God in action." I think that's beautiful — don't you? It speaks volumes to our situation. As we learned from the woman in prison, the law cannot forgive. It can only forgive if by some act of grace it is superceded by another law. Then it is again grace not law which is operative.

THE QUALITY OF GRACE SEEN IN JESUS

While grace was not totally unknown in the Old Testament Isaiah, Micah, Hosea, all had elements of it, as did the Psalms, it was nevertheless Jesus who gave it a quality people had not seen before.

It was so vital and fresh a thing that it had to be compared to the effervescent force of fermenting wine that would burst an old container. It had a quality that could not be proven by argument but had to be celebrated with a party when a lost boy came home. It was a grace that prompted a withering glance from Jesus to self-righteous men who with hidden lasciviousness dragged a poor woman before Him, who they claimed was a harlot but had probably been raped, that He might pronounce death by stoning. That glance of compassion to the woman and anger to the men backed by the simple words, "Whoever has no sin throw the first stone at her," sent these lip-smacking sadists off like whipped dogs to lick their wounds.

It was a grace that through the long night of questioning, buffeting, being lied to and lied about, being mocked and spat upon, then with the hot pinched nerve ends of crucified flesh sending searing flashes to the brain, could still do those gloriously gracious things which Jesus did on the Cross:

(a) Give assurance to a dying man on the Cross next to Him.
(b) Remember his mother who stood weeping at the foot of the Cross.
(c) Pray for those who did it to Him, "Father forgive them."
(d) And finally give the glorious assurance to us all that God was present in the midst of it, "Father into thy hands I commit my spirit."

This was the one moment in history when "the desperate tides of the whole world's anguish were forced through the channels of but a single heart."

Thus was borne out in one supreme life totally committed to expressing the love that was and is at the heart of God, such evidence of the reality and power of that love, that one who knew Him well and loved Him much could only say, "Out of His full store we have all received grace heaped upon grace." So may we be moved to pray with Catherine Arnott in the hymn —

> "O Christ, who died with arms outstretched in love
> for all who lift their faces to thy Cross
> Fill thou our lives with charity divine,
> Till thou and thine are all and self is lost."

GRACE AND THE COMMON LIFE

In conclusion let me tell you why this is not simply a subject for discussion by a miniscule elite with a theological bent. It has to do with the very stuff of which the common things and everyday relationships of life are made. Let me illustrate it this way.

I well recall one dull Saturday afternoon in 1928 when I was eight years of age. My father and brothers were all away and I found time heavy on my hands. I decided to go to the tool shed and make a cart. There was one tool I was told by my father not to use. It was a wooden mitre box which he had made. A mitre box is used for cutting pieces of wood accurately at different angles. As I worked at making the cart, to my horror I knocked the mitre box off the bench and broke a piece off one end of it. With shock, confusion and apprehension about what would happen when my father returned, I placed the tool back on the bench and set the broken piece in its place. You could scarcely see the crack! Maybe he will never notice it, I thought. He doesn't use it that often. I could tell him I picked the piece off the floor — that would be the truth! But all the time I knew what I had to do.

When my father arrived home that evening you can't imagine a more dutiful son. I ran out to help him unhitch the horse and unload the wagon. At some point in this burst of exuberance at being a dutiful son, I initiated a conversation which went something like this:

> "I was working in the tool shed this afternoon."
> "Were you?"
> "Yes, I was making a cart."

"How did you get along?"

"Not very well. I never finished it."

"Well, maybe another time — what else did you do?"

"You know that new mitre box you made, the one for cutting wood at different angles?"

"Yes, you mean the one I told you not to use?"

"Yes — yes — that's the one! (It's a wonder I didn't add, how'd you guess?)

"What about it?"

"I dropped it and it broke."

"You mean you dropped it, and you broke it?"

"Yes — I guess so — I'm sorry."

There was a long silence. We walked a little slower and then three fingers of a farmer's calloused left hand — he only had three on that hand having lost two in a sawmill as a youth — took a small boy's hand. The lamp my mother had placed in the kitchen window lighted our path. Then a firm but kind voice spoke, "I am sorry you did that, most of all I am sorry you did it when I told you not to — that box took a lot of time to make and came in mighty handy — so — (a long silence) you can help me and together we'll make a new one!"

The calloused hand felt warm and strong. The relationship of father to son and son to father never felt more secure. Love was in action — and it was sheer grace. But notice it was love that placed a responsibility on the recipient; it was not a depersonalized handout. "You will help me and together we will make a new one."

So God in His mercy looks upon us children. The law, given by Moses, we do not and cannot keep perfectly. The image in which God created us gets marred and sometimes broken. Then the father's voice says, "I am sorry you did that — I know you are sorry, too — so — tomorrow, today, right now — let's start together and we'll build again." It is grace heaped upon grace.

In the final analysis, sisters and brothers, that is not only an aspect of reality — it is the only ultimate reality — it is the only one that really matters.

Thanks be to God. Amen.

THE CHURCH AND POLITICS

"Religion begins in awe and ends in politics."

M. Buber.

Some women from Chile write:

"We're preparing more than pies
In the steaming kitchen of our eyes."

(From "On the Sidelines" about two children
stopped by soldiers and burned.)

"In politics the perception is the reality."

Senator Keith Davey.

Latin American proverb —

"For you who walk there is no road,
The road is made by walking."

All people are considered to be equal but, unfortunately, not all people are considered to be people.

"Ours is a sovereign nation
Bows to no foreign will
But whenever they cough in Washington
They spit on Parliament Hill."

Joe Wallace in "The Blasted Pine"

THE CHURCH AND POLITICS

Text: "Blessed is the nation whose God is the Lord."
Psalm 33:12

Shortly after I was elected Moderator, a journalist who writes for a Roman Catholic church paper phoned me. "I want to quote a statement to you and ask if you agree with it," he said. The statement was, "You can separate church and state, but you cannot separate God and good government." "I wish I had said that", I answered. He replied, "You did. You said it to me five years ago and I was just wondering if you still believed it."

Sometimes an interviewer looks at me, after I have spoken about the church's involvement in the society of which we are a part, and says something like, "Don't you think there is a danger of the church getting involved in politics?" The answer I give is that the church has been involved in politics ever since God said to Moses, "Go down and tell Pharaoh, let my people go." Not only that, but Moses backed up his words with his deeds. Pharaoh represented the political power of the day. Moses demonstrated, threatened, harassed and even practised civil disobedience in order to make his point.

I want to make three points in this address.

1. The church not only has a right to be involved — it has an obligation to be involved in the political processes of the nation.

2. We need to recognize the interdependent nature of that involvement — this will imply a respect for the

other elements of society with which we are involved in the process.

3. There is a spiritual basis for our ultimate hope, in spite of elusive goals, dawns deferred and hopes denied.

1. THE OBLIGATION FOR THE CHURCH TO BE INVOLVED

Some time ago I came out of the national offices of the church at 85 St. Clair Avenue to find a man walking up and down on the sidewalk accompanied by some of his friends. They were carrying placards. Earlier they had been at the Anglican Church headquarters at 600 Jarvis Street and at some of the Roman Catholic church offices. Their leader was a man whose name was Mr. Ken Long. The placards they carried and the literature they distributed bore such captions as, "Get the church out of politics"; "Preachers, why don't you stick to religion?"; "The church is a tool of the USSR". I spoke with Mr. Long and asked him what was back of the effort he was making and the concerns he was raising. He was direct and concise in his reply:

(a) The churches should leave politics to the politicians; economics to the economists; and stick to religion. Religion in this context equals saving souls — personal salvation — and nothing more.

(b) When the church gets involved in politics, it tends to have leftist leanings.

(c) The leadership of the church should always reflect the consensus of church thinking and should not depart from it.

I want to give attention to these three concerns raised by Mr. Ken Long and his associates.

NO-ONE IS NEUTRAL IN POLITICS

To begin with, no person is unpolitical or apolitical. We have neighbours on our street who are good, kindly folk who have lovely polite children, but they do not, because of religious convictions, have any community involvement. The Red Cross, the Heart Fund, the Terry Fox Fund, will knock of their doors in vain. The canvasser will be treated courteously, but informed that they "don't believe in supporting such causes." Furthermore, they refuse to allow the enumerator in either municipal, provincial or federal elections to register them to vote. They feel that the whole process is evil and is contrary to their religious convictions. They believe they are being neutral. But they are not. They are helping to decide issues by leaving the field to any demigod or political con artist who may happen along. Every one of us is part of the political process and influences that process for good or ill. The Jehovah Witnesses who refuse, for reasons of conscience, to give a blood transfusion to a child who may be dying of leukemia and, for the same reason, refuse to vote in an election, do not by this withdrawal leave medical affairs to the doctors or politics to the politicians. Withdrawal from the human scene solves nothing and is itself a vote for or against something.

POLITICAL MORALITY

If politics is, as some allege, "a dirty business", then we should not blame the politicians alone for that. Politics, like a stream, will rise to the level that the environment demands. Theology is too important to leave to the theologians. Health is too important to leave to the doctors. Lawmaking and enforcement are too important to leave to lawyers and politicians. Education is so vital a matter that we cannot entrust it to teachers and school trustees alone, and politics and economics cannot be left to the politicians and economists. The ebullient Harry Truman shouted to his advisors on one occasion, "Will someone please provide me with a one-armed economist and then he won't be able to say 'on the one hand, but then again on the other!' " Drinking a glass of water is a political act — the politicians decided from what source the water would be drawn, what purification process it would undergo before it entered the conduit system and whether it would contain chlorine or fluoride.

BISHOPS ON THE ECONOMY

The Roman Catholic Bishops were roundly criticized when they made a statement on the economy. The reason so many of the "common people" welcomed their statement was

because the bishops were filling a vacuum. They were offering
hope to people in a time of disillusionment, a light at the end
of the tunnel in a time of dark despair. Not only that, but the
very people who were most critical of them were the ones
whose policies brought us to such an impasse that it made the
bishops' statement necessary in the first place.

LEFTIST LEANINGS IN THE CHURCH

But let me turn now to the accusation that the church
in its involvement always places itself in a position with "leftist
leanings". This allegation needs to be taken seriously. What are
"leftist leanings"? The Oxford Dictionary defines "left" in a
variety of ways. The first is in the manner that any Boy Scout
or Girl Guide will understand immediately. "Left is the side of
a person's body that is westward when he faces north!" It may
also be the "wing of an army", or "political radicals collec-
tively speaking." But for our purposes, the definition that is
probably most relevant is the one which states, "left is the
advanced and innovative section of a philosophical school or
religious group." On that basis there were more leftists in the
Bible than there are in the leadership of the church today! On
that basis the prophet Isaiah and others, including Jesus, had
leftist tendencies.

RADICAL PROPHETS

Isaiah was a "radical" in the sense of the real meaning
of that word, which is "to get to the root of the issues", and
certainly he was "advanced and innovating." When speaking
in the name of Jehovah he said, "Is not this the fast that I
require — to loose the fetters of injustice, to untie the knots of
the yoke, to set free those who have been crushed?" He was
being both radical and innovative. Or again, when he cried,
"The wretched and the poor look for water and find none, but
I, the Lord, will give them an answer, I, the God of Israel, will
not forsake them." He denounced those who would "grind the
faces of the poor" and cried, "shame on you who add house to
house and land to land ... who for a bribe acquit the guilty and
deny justice."

Time is not sufficient to tell more of Moses who cried, "Let my people go", or Amos who denounced the speculators who would "sell the innocent for silver and the destitute for a pair of shoes", or those who "oppress the poor and crush the destitute", "who levy taxes on the poor" and "keep justice from the destitute."

And we need to realize that all these have their modern counterparts. What would Moses say about the taxes that are spent on the preparation of instruments of megadeath, while millions of children starve?

THE RADICALISM OF INCARNATION

Even the announcement of the Incarnation — the coming of God in Jesus Christ — has this radical cutting edge. Mary's song, commonly referred to as "The Magnificat", speaks of this.

> "The arrogant of heart and mind he has put to rout,
> he has brought down monarchs from their thrones,
> the humble have been lifted up,
> the hungry satisfied with good things,
> the rich he has sent empty away." (St. Luke 1)

Put that into modern terminology and it would read something like this:

> "The proud government and church bureaucrat he has
> put aside.
> The poor he has exalted.
> The bank and corporation president he has sent away
> and the welfare mother he has lifted up."

I am about ten minutes into this address. Do you realize in that ten minute period the nations of the world have spent ten million dollars on the preparations for nuclear war. With 1984 "doublespeak", they call it "peace keeping". Every second of that ten minutes two children have died of starvation on the planet Earth. If we take the mission of Jesus seriously, then it becomes *our* mission since the church according to St. Paul is, "the body of Jesus Christ".

Jesus continued the radicalism of his mother's prophecy when he set his chart and compass in the home synagogue. He said the Spirit of God was upon Him because he was sent to do three things:

> Preach the Gospel,
> Bring healing to the bruised and broken, and
> To set the prisoners free.

As the "body of Jesus Christ" we are called to this ministry and should not settle for less.

In making these references I am not using the Bible to "proof text" — a practice of which I disapprove. I am trying to indicate that a thread or trend runs through the Bible. It is this: God is on the side of the weak and powerless. God's concern is to liberate the oppressed and at the same time to stop the oppressor in his (or her) tracks in the hope that this may be the very moment of his (or her) own liberation.

Recently, I spent a day with nine "lifers" at Archambault Prison. I came to the conclusion that everyone in that set-up from the Solicitor General through the prison wardens, the guards in the corridors, as well as the prisoners behind the bars — are all prisoners of the system. Not only that, but we also are prisoners of that system because we put people away in the belief that that out of sight is out of mind. Other people have said it more eloquently than I am able to do, but I was convinced after a visit to South Africa that the whites are as much in need of liberation as the blacks — a fact which Bishop Tutu affirmed on a recent visit to Canada. They are in need of liberation from the cruel distortion of their own sense of values and of their estimate of the worth of human beings as reflected in the heinous doctrine of apartheid. They and we are in need of liberation from the nagging voice of conscience we cannot avoid, because we are all party to this discrimination. Through God's servants, the prophets, and through Jesus, God made plain which side the Divine Power is on and that this is the side which the disciples (the church) should be on. Further, in doing this, Jehovah addressed the political power of that day — the King. Our counterpart in a democracy is the Prime Minister, or the Leader of the Opposition, or the Cabinet.

THE "RELEVANCE" OF THE PROPHETS

Thirty-five years ago, Professor R.B.Y. Scott of United Theological College, Montreal, wrote a book on the prophets. It was entitled, "The Relevance of the Prophets", and it is still relevant. After more than two hundred pages of scholarly and sensitive commentary, Professor Scott points out that individual freedom depends upon "the responsible moral consciousness of a man or woman as a person." Then he goes on to say that this "creates the demand for civil and religious liberties ... and is part and parcel of the age long fight for full democratic liberty, and with it stands or falls." He continues, "The prophets are relevant to our modern social problems .... the slogans of democracy do not suffice. If we really care about freedom and justice, we must judge the worth and effectiveness of our present institutions by their actual results in human terms for *all* the people." He affirms that the difference between the under-privileged or the under-nourished and the comfortable is not due to the "moral superiority or greater mental capacity of the latter. It is due to the acceptance of conditions and the operation of factors which an aroused democracy can alter. Divine justice demands that they be altered." He goes on to state that at the time of the prophets, eight centuries before Christ, "the existing economic system" divided "people into conflicting groups .... It gives to individuals social power without social responsibility, and sets our hearts on a materialistic goal." In a similar manner, he affirms that "our political democracy, is largely nullified by the absence of a corresponding economic democracy". He concludes with this insight and this challenge: "To read the prophetic books is to feel .... that social and economic justice is the concern of religion. God is not outside the democratic struggle, but within it." I cannot help but recall here the words of Martin Buber, the Jewish scholar, when he said, "Religion begins in awe and ends in politics."

TWO DECADES LATER IT'S STILL TRUE

Of course we've come a long way since these words were written in 1944. Social democracy as referred to by Professor Scott has advanced. But it has advanced, in part at least, because there have been those who were prepared to dig for root causes and to challenge systemic power, which was sometimes systemic evil, or to be "the advanced or innovative section of a religious group" as the Oxford Dictionary defines "leftist". Also we need to note that the advance has often been more apparent than real and the gap between the rich and poor not only still exists, but in some cases has been growing wider year by year. The equation then is a simple one — God was involved in the political process. God is involved in the political process. The church, which is God's church, cannot get out of that process and be true to either its creator or itself.

In this I do not submit to a fundamentalism of either the right or the left. And fundamentalists can be found in both camps. I do not want to see my church go in a 90 degree turn either right or left. At present we are more in danger of going right than we are of going left. But what I do want to see the church be is a body of people who take seriously the demands of the gospel and the demands of the prophets of Israel in regard to these very things of which I have been speaking.

IS MERE CONSENSUS THE ANSWER?

Let me touch briefly on the third point which was made by the largely unidentified group which picketed United Church House some months ago. The opinion was expressed that the leadership of the church "does not reflect fully enough, and ought not to be in conflict with the opinion of the membership of the church."

So often when I am involved in such things as peace walks, demonstrations against the cruise missile, urging the Prime Minister to become involved in building bridges between the USSR and the USA, and things of that nature, people will say to me that I do not reflect the total opinion of the total membership of the United Church of Canada. I don't think I ever suggested, pretended, or believed I did. If one were going to wait until one reflected the opinion of 100% of the membership of the United Church of Canada — or any other church, for that matter — one would remain silent the rest of one's life.

RESPECT FOR OPINION OF OTHERS

But there is a salutary warning to the credit of those who raised this question that we need to take seriously. Part of it is that those of us who have strong convictions about some of these issues which we believe are derived from our understanding of the prophets and the gospel, need to present our case in such a way that we show respect for the rights of others. We need to avoid the hazard of becoming like a college I read about in the United States, which sent a brochure around the state in which it was located, urging people to send their children to this "Christian centre of learning". The *piece de resistance* of their appeal was that this college "is situated seven miles from any known form of sin!" Obviously the greatest sin of all was right in the midst of it — the sin of pride. While we need to realize, as the French theologian Jacques Ellul has said, "all institutions — including the church — come under the judgments of God", nevertheless we must not compromise our integrity by the affirmations which we make or the positions which we adopt. The notion some people have that every decision the church or its leaders make ought to be done on the basis of some kind of consensus or referendum does not have any basis in gospel or in the tradition of the church. Caiaphas, who wanted Jesus put to death, spoke for more people than Nicodemus did. Pilate responded to the consensus of the people and ordered Jesus put to death; in less than twenty-four hours he washed his hands of the whole affair. Martin Luther, over 500 years ago, did not submit the thesis which he hammered on the church door in Wittenberg to popular vote before declaring where he stood. Obviously, if Jesus had submitted his decision to go the way of the Cross to a vote by the disciples, he would not have died. Peter followed the lead of the Holy Spirit, not George Gallop when he admitted Cornelius to Church fellowship.

CHRISTIAN COURAGE IN
A COMMUNIST COUNTRY

One of the gutsiest statements I have heard about discipleship in the last few years was one night when I was attending a meeting of the equivalent of a United Church session in the Lutheran Church of the Evangelical Union in the German Democratic Republic. Recall now that I am talking about the church in a communist country. I asked the group through an interpreter what it was like to be the church under communism. Following a brief silence, an eighteen year old woman replied. This is what she said: "To be the church in our country you have to be a Gethsemane Church. That is, you have to be constantly asking yourself 'what is God's will for me?', and say, 'Lord, not my will but thine be done.' "In addition to that," she said, "You have to have in your mind the words which I have in capital letters on the wall of my room and they are these: 'We know that God can do anything. But there is one thing God cannot do. God cannot forsake those who fully trust him.' " When I listened to those words I knew in my heart that the church of Jesus Christ in the German Democratic Republic has a future. It is from my recollection of these qualities of faith demonstrated in the lives of so many of God's saints today that I take much inspiration. It is this that keeps me involved and will not allow me to turn back from praying, walking, talking and working for peace with justice and the rights of women and men to be treated as children of God, made in His image, wherever they are on the face of the earth. To do this the Church must be involved at the political level. You can, and indeed in a representative democracy you *must* separate Church and state, but you cannot separate God and good government.

Thanks be to God. Amen.

TELLING MY STORY — SHARING MY FAITH

Prayer:

God we know you care about us and for us and
for all your children.
Your love is like that of a mother whose prayers
never cease; it is like that of a father whose
concern is constant.

God some people wonder if you care
about them
or their children
or your world.

They've seen their hopes shattered,
– their dreams crumble to dust,
– their vision blurred and distorted,
– their strength is sapped
and the arms hang down,
– the feet move as if lead weights
were fastened to them.

Lord, empower them and us by your spirit,
– embolden us by your presence,
– forgive us by your grace,
– recreate us by your love.

So empowered, emboldened, forgiven and
recreated, send us forth to do your will — in the
name of our enabling Christ. Amen.

TELLING MY STORY —
SHARING MY FAITH

Scripture: St. Luke 2: 41-52
Ephesians 2: 1-10

BEGINNINGS

I was at a meeting one time where we were asked to
think back to the earliest recollection we had of being persons.
This meant recalling the first time I had a consciousness of
being human and an awareness of the world around me.

In doing this, the earliest recollection I had was of two
occasions. Both of these must have taken place before I was
five years of age because they happened before I started to
school. On the first occasion I recall coming from Salem Presbyterian Church, Picton Co., Nova Scotia. It was wintertime
and the family was being transported in the box sleigh. The
box sleigh was a large wooden sleigh which could several persons. Being the youngest of a family of five children I was
wrapped up warmly in a buffalo rug in the back corner of the
sleigh, while my older brothers and sister were jumping in and
out of the sleigh throwing snowballs at each other and just
having a good time.

The second occasion was the first year that my brother,
next older than myself, started to school. We were very close
to each other and I missed him a lot when he went off to
school. One morning, about 10 o'clock, I went up to the school-
house which was near to our home, knocked on the door of

the school and asked the teacher if my brother could come out to play with me. She, of course, told me he could not and that I must not interrupt the school classes in this manner. I recall that my next move was to go out on the road, gather up a handful of small stones and then go back and throw them one at a time at the side of the school! At this point the teacher came out and, in no uncertain terms, told me to go home or else suffer dire consequences. Someone commenting on this said, "That sounds just like Clarke MacDonald. He's getting aid and comfort from the church and throwing stones at an establishment where he thinks his brother is being held a prisoner!"

SMALL BUT SECURE

By now you get the picture of a boy who was brought up in a small community and who felt secure in a family circle where church and school were held in high regard. Add to this the ingredients of hard work, thrift during the depression, as well as concern about one's neighbours, and you have a fairly accurate picture of what actually obtained. The community was small, the neighbours were kind and one somehow got the idea that as long as there was a King on the throne in England and God was a Presbyterian everything would be well! When I went to school I had a feeling of security in knowing that my oldest brother was the strongest boy there and could come to my defence if needed!

But back to matters of faith. There was a reason for the passages of scripture read at the beginning of this service. In St. Luke 2 we have the story of the boy Jesus. I was attracted by the way faith seemed so natural to him. As a boy, belief came easily to me — questions and doubts were to come later. In the meantime I enjoyed my religion. People were kind and I assumed that the whole world would be like the little bit of it in which I lived and moved and had my being, where everyone was supportive and thoughtful. Of course that was naive. I thought if you did your lessons and chores, said your prayers and went to church you would be OK. My world was bounded by Pictou on the north, New Glasgow on the east, Truro on the south, and lots of trees and hills on the west beyond which there was a place called Amherst to which we went once a year to the Maritime Winter Fair. Life was simple — small was beautiful — God was love. What more could one want!

COMPLEXITY SETS IN

But soon life became more complex. I read history and studied about Europe, about wars, about the French Revolution, about the American War of Independence, about the Battle on the Plains of Abraham, or at Louisbourg or at Port Royal and all of this produced a mixture of admiration and fear. There was admiration for the courage of those brave men who went off to battle and fear at the realization that something which lay deep in the heart of man had caused the strife. The violence and deceit were things new in my perspective of thought. The simple, small, beautiful world became monstrous and forbidding. Yet lights of hope began to flash through, largely due to the missionaries. Their stories of light and darkness were highlighted by the work of the Women's Missionary Society which met frequently in my mother's living room and provided a double joy. The sandwiches and cakes left over, after they had met, were a bonus to the enjoyment I took in the stories I heard and read about distant places and that fascinated me. I remember about the age of five hearing a missionary for the first time. He was Dr. Cock of India, whom I listened to in the Presbyterian Church at Salem. After that I thrilled to the stories of Sid Gilchrist in Africa, Forbes in China and MacKenzie in Korea.

Then came a time for inner turmoil. What had earlier been natural to me now became more forced and compulsive. The concept of Jesus the "pal", Jesus the "friend" was replaced by the notion of Jesus as "the power". The power to destroy as well as the power to build. "Duty thou stern daughter of the voice of God" became very real to me. Fear grabbed me. "What if I didn't measure up?" Dr. Ian McKinnon, Hugh Irwin, Calder Fraser, Rev. Ward MacLean, all ministers in my boyhood preached sermons about a God of Love. Yet pictures I had seen in a copy of Pilgrim's Progress showing the damned in a pit with their pale and anxious faces surrounded by walls of flame and asbestos-suited guards at the door with pitch forks to prevent escape, terrified me. I heard about a sermon preached by a man named Jonathan Edwards called "Sinners In the Hands of An Angry God" in which he depicted God dangling sinners over the pit of fire. This was all very vivid in my boyish mind and very frightening. That's why later I determined that while I would be honest about interpreting the moral order of the universe, I would never, but never, allow my own or anyone else's child to be frightened by a picture painted by me of a vicious and retaliating God. Yet it was not all gloom and doom.

COMMITMENT — THE TURNING POINT

Life at this time was held together by a home where there was love, by a church where ministers were the kind I could look up to and respect. The turning point was in October, 1934. It was Saturday night, we were gathered for "preparatory services" before Holy Communion. The service was in the old community dance hall where our congregation used to gather on Sunday afternoon. I'll never forget that night. It meant more to me than my ordination for ministry. At ordination nine years later, I committed my life to a particular ministry within my commitment to Christ. That Saturday night *I committed my life to Christ*. I said, "yes," to Him and somehow even then I had the feeling that life would never be the same again — and it has not been but I had no idea how strangely different it would be.

I had two ideas about what I wanted to be. I wanted to be either a train engineer or a minister. When my uncle, who worked on the railway, told me I would have to shovel coal from five to ten years before becoming an engineer, my enthusiasm for that vocation began to wane! I've talked to ministers who told me that their parents practically drove them into the ministry and they later resented it. It is not long since I spoke with a Roman Catholic priest and a Protestant minister both of whom felt this way. It was not so in my case, it was a personal commitment. The encouragement was there and once the decision was made I had support all the way.

NEW VISTAS AND NEW PROBLEMS

So it was off to college where new worlds opened up to me, the world of books and the world of people. The first week I was there I heard Dr. John R. Mott. He had just returned from a world tour and opened up all kinds of vistas to my imagination. I was taking Arts at Dalhousie at the time, but I never missed a visiting lecturer at Pine Hill. There I heard Dr. John Coburn on temperance, Dr. James Endicott on China, Dr. Liston Pope on theology, Dr. Gilchrist on Africa, and Dr. J. D. N. MacDonald on cooperatives. An older student said to me, "Clarke, do you realize you have four years in Arts and three in theology. You're going to be mighty tired listening to people talk about theology before you leave here." He could not have been more wrong. Right up to the present I never grow weary of discussing relevant, practical theology and its application to all of life. I despise theology that is nit-picking, irrelevant, obtuse and lifeless, but I thrill to a theology that is living, vital and challenging.

Yet it wasn't easy going. Aspects of the angry God I had heard about still haunted me. I was not as good a student as some of my friends were. I couldn't pray like the student who came to the United Church from the Methodist Church in England, and I didn't think I would ever be able to preach like him either. My grades were only average and sometimes less than average. The law of perfection was there but I could not attain unto it. I even thought I should be able to live like St. Paul! I poured over his letters, I actually missed meals on more than one occasion in order to try to find out what the driving power of his life was and how it could be attained. So "the dark night of the soul," settled in upon my life. I thought I would quit the ministry. I wrestled with doubts, fears, hopes that seemed elusive and dawns that were constantly deferred.

ANOTHER TURN IN THE ROAD

Then one night, during the war, I was working at the Salvation Army Hostel for service men on Hollis Street in Halifax. It was Saturday night; my task was to be there from 7 o'clock at night until 7 o'clock in the morning. I assigned beds to the sailors, soldiers and airmen who came to stay for the night and kept the coffee urn filled. In addition to my personal search, I was also engaged in New Testament studies as part of my course at Pine Hill College. I took my Bible with me to do some reading in the hours between 1 a.m. and 4 a.m. when there was very little work to do. It was about 4 o'clock and I was reading in Saint Paul's letter to the Ephesians in chapter two. I read the eighth verse, "For by grace are ye saved through faith, and that not of yourselves, it is the gift of God." I paused after I read it and I read it again, then I read it for the third time. As if by a flash of forked lightning, the darkness was illumined. I saw something which was so simple I could hardly believe it, yet so true I had to repeat it over and over again "not of yourself" — "not of yourself" — "grace" — "grace". I had read John Oman — "Grace is the Love of God in action." It was stupid of me not to have seen it before. The things I was worried about seemed as nothing now. I didn't have to get as good marks as any other student, but simply to get as good as I was able. It didn't matter if I couldn't pray and preach like the probation trained Methodist from Britain — I had only to do my best. Salvation did not depend on keeping the law — it was not by works because then I could boast about it — it was by grace. That happened at 4 a.m. on Sunday; my shift was over at 7 a.m. I suspect that morning as I went from bunk to bunk awakening the men and then pouring the cups of coffee, that there was a spring in my step and a lilt in my voice that had not been there before. I know there was a joy in my heart that I had never known before. As I went back to Pine Hill residence, dawn was breaking over Point Pleasant Park and it was also breaking over my spirit — but the fog horns were still blaring in the distance warning sailors of unseen shoals, a fitting reminder to me that all would not be sweetness and light. It was as if God was saying, "You're on the right track but there is tough going ahead." When I got back to the residence I dropped in at the residence chapel for Sunday morning prayers. Was it coincidence that the first hymn was Toplady's:

> "Not the labour of my hands
> Can fulfil the laws demands
> Could my zeal no respite know,
> Could my tears forever flow,

All for sin could not atone,
Thou must save and Thou alone."

I was embarked on what I call a Christo-centric faith and there was no turning back.

But that was only the beginning. God won't leave us at rest for long. We settle down and He pokes and nudges at us always telling us to get going, to break new ground. Look at the symbols used in the Bible — a garden — that means growth; an ark for the saving of the people — that means voyaging; a sign on the door post so that when you move, you take it with you. When Joseph was asleep God nudged him in the middle of the night and told him to take his wife and child and flee from Bethlehem into a strange land called Egypt. That child became a pilgrim who moved from city to city, from town to town, from province to province, using boat, sandalled foot and donkey back to make his journey. Finally, when they thought they had done him in on a cross and placed his body in a tomb with a heavy stone against it, the open door of that tomb became a symbol of a God who moves the seal of death. So that night God told me to get going in the ministry I had thought of leaving.

A HAPPY AND FAR REACHING INTERLUDE

Then about a year later there was a happy interlude; again it was Saturday night. I went to Prince Edward Island to preach and that night there was a heavy snow storm. Trains and ferry boats were "hung up", as they say, because of ice in the Strait. I knew I would not get back to Pine Hill College in time anyway, so I decided to stay over for an extra day and ask a girl there, who had been my friend for a year, if she would marry me! I stayed, she agreed, and I felt at last I had done something right. Little did we know how profound would be the theological implications of our marriage, in addition to the anticipated joys and struggles together. We did not know we would experience the death of two children, the joy of two others who have grown into manhood and the added grace note of a "chosen" daughter as well as the many other experiences with which, "the web of time is woven." These experiences were a large factor in making us — our marriage — our home and our life together what it is.

A SECOND FUNNEL FOR MINISTRY

While in training for the ministry, I had been taught that the preaching, the sacraments and the visitation of the people were central. But I also knew that for me there had to be another dimension. Some years later Dr. Donald Soper gave me a word for it. He called it "my second funnel." In his case it was the Hyde Park Corner ministry — the Labour Party and subsequently the House of Lords. For me it was the Co-op — Credit Union movement, the Labour Union in Sydney and the Soap Box Forum in Allan Gardens Park, Toronto.

Long before Pope John helped to break down the walls of dogma that separated Roman Catholics and Protestants, I went with Dr. M. M. Coady, Mr. Mac McDonnell, Joe Chisholm, Father Topshee, Rev. J. D. N. MacDonald and others, footslogging through to schools and halls in places like Rear Judique, Whycocomagh and Mabou, Cape Breton. I'll never forget one night when a United Church elder from Whycocomagh came to me in Mabou Hall and shaking my hand said with a fervent tone: "Thank God, at last. I've been praying that some of our ministers would see the need to get involved at this level." That was the beginning of a ministry of involvement which today is marked by concern that the church be responsibly involved in the things that touch the lives of men and women in the world where they are working and playing and birthing and dying. It prepared me to handle the criticisms I get now, for instance, from supporters of the brewers telling me the Church should mind its own business — which means, leave us alone, and let us make our profits — forget about death on the highway and murder in the homes from liquor-crazed minds; or the petroleum companies that object to our way of defending native people's rights; or politicians who tell us that we can become a nation of gamblers and still maintain our integrity. All this was part of the preparation for the daily diet that now comes my way from across the nation.

THE BASIC SYMBOL OF COMMITMENT REMAINS

But it is all the outgrowth of what happened that Saturday night when I was fourteen years of age. Symbols may become stronger in memory than they appear at the first encounter. The symbol of the exodus of the Jews, the symbol of the Bread and the Cup to the Christian, the symbol of the flag to the patriot, intensify with the passage of time. In the same way the symbol — which was also the reality — on that Saturday night at the front of the community dance hall when Rev. Ward MacLean said to a fourteen year old boy, "Do you confess Jesus Christ as Saviour and Lord and will you seek earnestly the peace and welfare of the church of God?" and I replied: "I will do so, the Lord be my helper", abides to this time. That's the symbol of my relationship to God. How it has been worked out since is part of His design and His ability to use me in spite of my failures and mistakes.

I will close with this illustration and tribute because it is a memorable part of my faith story and is also symbolic of a very powerful influence in my life.

It was August 4th, 1973. My wife Muriel, our daughter Rose and I were on our way from Berwick camp to Cape Breton, where I was to preach next day. Again it was a Saturday. We stopped at Green Hill, Pictou Co., to visit my parents. We knew mother was unwell and we found her in much pain waiting for word when a hospital bed would be available for her. We had the inevitable cup of tea that went with any visit to my parents' house. I was helping mother from her wheelchair back to her couch in the living room. As I lowered her to the pillow she said: "Well, Clarke boy," (when she said: "Clarke boy", I knew something important was about to be spoken), "I'm slipping, I'm slipping fast." With that human resistance to facing reality — especially the reality of death — I said: "Well, mom, we're all getting twenty-four hours older every day." Even as I said the words I began to burn inwardly with shame. Here was my mother trying to tell me something as final as death, as ultimate as God Himself and I was mouthing triteness and shallowness. So I rebuked myself and went on, "But the important thing, Mother," I said, "is what you have always taught your children. That it does not matter what happens to us in life, God is always with us, and He's here now." "That's right, son," she said, "and it's a good thing it is that way." Apart from saying, "Goodbye" those were the last words that passed between my mother and me.

This is not the end of my faith story but it is the conclusion of this chapter. The rest is in the hands of God I like it to be that way.

Thanks be to God. Amen.

PROPHETS THEN AND PROPHETS NOW

The Gospel to All Realms of Life

In the Bible, religion was never limited to the temple or isolated from daily life (Hosea 6:4-6; Isaiah 58:6-7). The teaching of Jesus on the kingdom of God is a clear reference to God's loving lordship over all human history. We cannot limit our witness to a supposedly private area of life. The lordship of Christ is to be proclaimed to all realms of life.

In the fulfilment of its vocation, the church is called to announce Good News in Jesus Christ, forgiveness, hope, a new heaven and a new earth; to denounce powers and principalities, sin and injustice; to console the widows and orphans, healing, restoring the broken-hearted; and to celebrate life in the midst of death. In carrying out these tasks, churches may meet limitations, constraints, even persecution from prevailing powers which pretend to have final authority over the life and destiny of people.

In some countries there is pressure to limit religion to the private life of the believer, to assert that freedom to believe should be enough. The Christian faith challenges that assumption. The church claims the right and the duty to exist publicly, visibly, and to address itself openly to issues of human concern.

Reprinted from the World Council of Churches
Commission on World Mission and Evangelism.

95

PROPHETS THEN AND
PROPHETS NOW

Text: "Thus says the Lord..."

Amos 3:12

     Beginning to prepare a message about the prophets is, I think, like starting to paint on a huge canvas. What is the central theme you want to emphasize? Where do you begin? What are the colours you want to bring out in bold relief? We have listened again and again to readings from and about the prophets. The names are familiar — Moses, Isaiah, Jeremiah, Amos, and a host of others. In the eleventh chapter of the Book of Hebrews in the New Testament the writer takes us through the prophets' Hall of Fame. Both men and women, some well known, others not so, Enoch, Noah, Abraham, Sarah, even Rahab, the prostitute; and then the writer says, "Should I go on ... there isn't time ...". If I were to update that list and speak of this century, likewise there would not be time. Schweitzer, Bonhoeffer, Nellie McClung, Pope John XXIII, Martin Luther King, Rev. Lydia Gruchy, Bishop Tutu, Mother Theresa ..... The extent of the subject, plus the limitations of time and of the speaker, prevent an exhaustive treatment of the theme of prophets, both then and now. Also, I want to avoid the pitfall of a student who put a note at the end of his philosophy exam paper, "I find it difficult to answer the riddle of the universe in two hours." The professor returned the paper to the student with this note, "If I had known you had the answer, I would have given you more time!" Any adequate treatment of this subject will always require more time. It has to begin with a reference to the prophets of Israel who were accorded a role of significance unparalleled in the history of the Hebrews, or in any other history for that matter. These prophets had an understanding of events which saw these only in terms of a divine purpose and a divine will. While prophecy begins with Moses, yet in the annals of the Old Testament there is a period of about 200 years which were the peak years of prophecy in Israel. These saw the emergence of the notables — Amos, Hosea, Isaiah, Micah, Jeremiah, Ezekiel and Deutero-Isaiah.

One could paraphrase the words of Alfred Tennyson about John Milton to apply to the prophets of Israel:

"O mightly mouthed inventor of harmonies,
O skilled to sing of Time or Eternity,
God gifted organ voice of Israel,
Prophets — a name to resound for ages."

THE WORD — "PROPHET"

The Hebrew word "prophet" appears some 300 times in the Old Testament. This includes, of course, reference to both true and false, primitive and sophisticated prophets. In the New Testament the office of prophet is retained for a much smaller number. John the Baptist was definitely thought of as a prophet. Jesus was considered by many to be a prophet as well. St. Paul saw prophecy as a viable and justifiable continuance of the prophecy of the Old Testament. Judas and Silas, the Apostles, were defined in this role. Paul was opposed to extreme aspects that often crept into prophecy. "Though I have the gift of prophecy and understand all mysteries and have not love — I am nothing." He saw prophecy as part of the divinely imparted spirit of God in interpretation of the meaning of history. He would, I am sure, categorically disown much of that which passes for prophecy in some circles today.

While the origin of the Hebrew word for "prophet" is lost in antiquity, yet like most things the Hebrew touched, the word came to carry an ultimate and divine intent. The Arabic word "Pi-el" — "prophet" — is related to the Arabic word meaning "to call" or "to announce". The prophets then were ones who announced the purpose and activity of God. They were forthtellers not foretellers of this activity. Moving from the Hebrew to the Greek understanding of prophecy is like moving from bright sunshine to grey shadows.

In the Greek tradition the prophet had more of the sense of divination and was designated an interpreter of divine oracles. The sanctuary of Apollo at Delphi was the centre of divination in classical antiquity. In these pagan centres young women, known as the "Pythia", spoke to mortals in the name of the god whose message was being transmitted. Their words, usually unintelligible, were translated by priestly attendants referred to as prophets. The temples and shrines of the ancient Middle East were filled with such soothsayers.

Some of the Hebrew prophets were conscious of this soothsaying and seer-telling role. They did not like this perverted notion of "fore-telling" the purposes of God so they referred to these soothsayers as false prophets. They disassociated themselves from them. Amos, for example, would have nothing to do with them and went to the extreme of saying, "I was no prophet, nor the son of a prophet." Thus he disassociated himself from the prophetic guild. He crossed their picket lines, so to speak. To the Hebrew, Moses was the prophet par-excellence, "there has never yet arisen a prophet like Moses, whom the Lord knew face to face." It is small wonder that some found the reference to Jesus — "a greater than Moses is here", to be quite offensive.

WOMEN IN PROPHECY

Although none of the prophetic books are named after women, and women as a rule don't fare too well in the Old Testament record — since it is largely the record of the activity of men written by men — yet some of them are prophetesses in their own right and were so recognized. When the children of Israel crossed the water dry-sandalled and the horsemen of Pharaoh found themselves covered with the swirling waters, Miriam "the prophetess" was one of the first to notice what had taken place. She was in raptures of delight at the unhappy fate of their former taskmasters. She took up her tambourine, and all the women followed her, dancing to the sound of the tambourine and Miriam sang them this refrain. "Sing to the

Lord for he has risen up in triumph, the horse and his rider he has hurled into the sea." She was obviously the one who was the first with her sensitive feminine insight to observe the victory which God had already achieved for Israel in its liberation movement. It is not without significance that it was a woman who first celebrated the liberation of Israel from bondage in Egypt and it was a woman who was chosen as bearer of the One whom Christians would claim was the liberator, of those who believe, from the bondage of sin.

Deborah, the wife of Lappidoth, was a prophetess as well as being a judge in Israel. She was a sort of Israelitish version of a combination of Charlotte Whitton, Barbara Amiel and Margaret Thatcher! Seated one day beneath the palm trees at Ramah dispensing justice, she suddenly sent for Barak, commander of the troops. She gave him a terse message from the Lord, "This is the command of the Lord God of Israel, go and do battle against Sisera (Jablin's commander) with all his chariots, and his rabble, and I will deliver them into your hands." Now this man Barak was a first class wimp! He replied to Deborah, "If you go with me, I will go; if you will not, neither will I." "Certainly, I will go with you", she replied, "but this venture will bring you no glory, because the Lord will leave Sisera to fall into the hands of a woman." Deborah did, Barak did — and the Lord did. For Sisera was defeated and Jael, Heber the Caananite's wife, was given custody over him. She "made him comfortable in her tent." Now let your imagination go to work on that scene! Sisera asked for water and she gave him warm milk — spiked I assume with you know what. It would be interesting if the Bible afforded us a record of all the byplay which took place here. Jael conned this great general into believing she would keep watch for him while he slept. As a matter of fact she did watch him until he dozed off and then straight away drove a tent peg through his skull. This part of the story should be marked "for restricted viewing." It concludes, "his brains oozed out on the ground, his limbs twitched and he died." Regardless of this, Deborah's place in prophecy has been confirmed.

It is, however, women like Anna — the prophetess — who redeemed the situation by bringing a sensitive and gentle factor to the equation. She was with Simeon the prophet, and was like him, "waiting for the consolations of Israel," when the baby Jesus was dedicated in the temple. She echoed Simeon's words, "Lord now lettest Thou thy servant depart in peace ...." and her arms, after Mary's, were probably the first woman's to cradle the One whom, in the Creed, Christians dare to call "very God of very God."

ABERRATIONS OF THE PROPHETIC ROLE

It is worth noting that there were some ecstatic aberrations of prophecy recorded in the Bible. When Saul went beserk with jealous rage against David and tried to skewer him to the palace wall with his spear, David wisely made friends with his heels. He took off for shelter to his friend, Samuel of Rahmah, at Naioth. Saul sent a company of soldiers to bring him back. When they arrived at Naioth they found Samuel in a trance and leading the people in ecstacy and in prophecy. Everyone was caught up in the spirit of it, including Saul's soldiers. They went into rapturous ecstacy and they also went AWOL and failed to return with their man. Saul sent two more posses who met the same fate, so at last he decided to go himself. Little did he realize that he too would come under the spell of the moment and "the spirit of God came on Saul" and he, too, went into rapture. With the others he did a simulation of the last scene of the musical "Hair". Divesting themselves of their garments, they lay naked before Samuel all day and all night. While Saul and the boys were lying around in the "altogether but altogether", David sensing the danger slipped out of his trance and into his pants and took off for his friend, Jonathan, who helped him escape this second time. This was the beginning of a mushrooming of cultists of prophetic types and ecstatic bands who roamed the country. We are not without their counterparts today. In fact some of the electronic evangelists would quality — especially the one who takes five minutes to speak of salvation and fifty minutes to plead for money.

MARKS OF PROPHETS — COURAGE

Whether it was Jeremiah challenging his countrymen and being put in prison and thrown into a pit for his prophecy, or Peter and John at the gate, called beautiful, of the temple saying, "we cannot but speak of those things which we have seen and heard", courage was a hallmark of the prophets. But let us be sure that we know exactly what we mean at this point. It is courage, not cockiness, we are talking about. It is grace under pressure, not abrasive self assurance. It is humility with strength, not arrogance. We are speaking of humbly acknowledging the majesty and omnipotence of God and recognizing that we are merely instruments in his hand. It may be even what I heard one Rabbi call "transcendent humanism" — with the emphasis on transcendent .

When Bishop Tutu closed his moving address to thirty-five hundred people in St. Paul's Anglican Church, Toronto, with the oft repeated words "Help me please help me ....." and spoke these words over and over again, one became conscious of the vulnerability of a man should he ever be separated from the source of his courage in his relationship to the eternal God. He was praying at one and the same time to God for courage and strength and beseeching us for support and the willingness to stand with him.

FORTHTELLERS

The prophets, as has been indicated, were not foretellers but forthtellers of the will of God. They were open to God's spirit and to God's direction. They often went against the mainstream of society. They were not running a popularity contest. The story is told of two men who were standing by the bank of the Thames River which runs through London, England, watching a swimmer out in the water. One man remarked, "Do you see that Quaker who is swimming out there?" The other replied, "I see the swimmer, but how can you tell a person is a Quaker by the way he swims?" His friend replied, "It is obvious that he is a Quaker because he is swimming against the current!" A prophet may sometimes stand alone or he/she may stand with the collective. Cora Aquino, of the Phillipines, may well be considered a prophetess in her own right. She forthtold the downfall of Marcus and then with a collective of people began a courageous uphill climb to the position of leadership in her country. What she began alone as the widow of the murdered leader of the opposition, became a movement of the people and resulted in a startling turn-around in the future of the leadership of that country. But a corollary of this is that the prophet must evaluate, reflect, correct, strategise anew to be sure that he/she is on track. A strategy that worked for Amos had to be revised and adapted to meet the needs confronted by Martin Luther King.

A BACKGROUND OF HOPE

The prophet always both works against a background of hope and emphasizes the hope that comes to people who work and plan within God's will for them. The "ark" to the saving of the people; the cloud by day and the pillar of fire by night; manna in the desert; angels ministering to Jesus in the wilderness — all of these remind us that we are not alone. The two major festivals of two living faiths, that of the "Passover" of the Jews and "Easter" for the Christians are sometimes concurrent on the calendar and this emphasizes the reality of their meaning. The Passover was the time when the homes of the Hebrew were passed over and escaped the scourge of death. On the other hand, the empty tomb with its message of hope to Christian believers is, as well, a message of hope to those who are imprisoned in their own folly.

THE QUESTION — THE BOTTOM LINE QUESTION
IS — SHOULD THE CHURCH BE PROPHETIC?
IS THE CHURCH BEING PROPHETIC?
WHAT STRATEGY SHOULD THE CHURCH
FOLLOW TO BE PROPHETIC?

The answer to the first question should be obvious to anyone well acquainted with the writings of the prophets of Israel and the New Testament. What alternative but to "forth tell" the will of God? Courage! And insight into the affairs of people and nations! When Isaiah saw the wicked nation to the north — Assyria — as the instrument of God to bring Israel to her senses, he was reading the signs of the times. One of the main reasons and basic justifications for our concern about peace with justice in our time is precisely the same thing. The nations of the west, some of whom stamp "in God we Trust" on their coins and many of whom affirm God in their constitutions, have no alternative but to say "the Lord has spoken who can but prophesy?" At the same time we need to note the thread that runs through the Bible telling us that God is on the side of the oppressed — God is on the side of the poor — God is on the side of the marginalized. This does not mean that God is not with the favoured ones. It does mean that God is calling us all to stand for justice and truth. As to the strategies, the church should use every strategy that it can at the same time as it maintains its integrity as the body of Jesus Christ. The cry of God through Moses to the oppressor, "let my people go" could be repeated in fifty different countries today. The cry of Amos against those who would "sell the innocent for a pair of shoes" and those who "levy taxes on the poor" could be levelled against any nation today that is taxing people exorbitantly to prepare its war machine, while at the same time its people are without food, shelter and the common amenities of life. This will require a vision on our part. Without claiming to be a member of the prophetic guild and in a small way, I want to contribute to that sense of vision. On a Saturday night as I was completing a sermon for the next day, I wrote these words which I now share with you:

I have a vision — of a church where people are welcomed because they are persons, not because they have a credal passport.

I have a vision — of a church where Christ is exalted in the totality of what he was, and people are encouraged to respond to Christ because of what he is to them now.

I have a vision — of a church where ministry is considered valid because it is born of the Spirit and bears the fruit of the spirit.

I have a vision — of a church which is not a museum for the outworn remains of a fossilized piety, but a haven for the very weary and very human: a place of healing for the bruised and broken, a place where there is the laughter of children, the brightness of joyous music, the sure confidence of the Word of God, and exuberance of youth, the strength of women and men, the counsel of age, the power of the spirit of the living God and the power of the very common and very real love for one another.

It is to make real that sort of vision and that kind of church that I am committed.

Thanks be to God. Amen.

PLANET AT THE CROSSROADS

Text: "Behold I set before you life and death,
therefore, choose life."

Deut: 30:19

Did Jonathan Schell know about this text? I have no
way of knowing for certain, but when I read the concluding
chapter of his book, "Fate of the Earth" I am led to believe he
knew this passage of scripture well. In his book, hailed by
some reviewers as the most significant one to appear for some
decades, if not in this century, he clearly sets before us, in our
generation, the choice between life and death. He concludes
his thought-provoking analysis with these words: "Two paths
lie before us. One leads to death, the other to life. If we choose
the first path, if we numbly refuse to acknowledge the nearness of extinction, all the while increasing our preparations to
bring it about, then we in effect become the allies of death. On
the other hand, if we reject our doom, and bend our efforts
towards survival ..... if we arouse ourselves to the peril and act
to forestall it, making ourselves the allies of life ..... then the
anaesthetic fog will lift: our vision, no longer straining not to
see the obvious, will sharpen; our will, finding secure ground
to build on, will be restored; and we will take full and clear
possession of life again. One day ..... and it is hard to believe
that it will not be soon ..... we will make our choice. Either we
will sink into the final coma and end it all or, as I trust and
believe, we will awaken to the truth of our peril, a truth as
great as life itself ..... we will break through the layers of our

denials, put aside our faint-hearted excuses, and rise up to cleanse the earth of nuclear weapons."

I do not wish to depress your thoughts by giving you verbal pictures of the madness of the world in which we live, where some 800m billion dollars a year are spent on armaments. But if we think Cherynobal was a tragedy — and it was; if we think Hiroshima was a living hell — and it was; if we think the murder of six million Jews by the Nazis was one of the lowest points in human morality and it was .... then let us realize that all of these, horrible though they were, and this is not to minimize any of them, were but a prelude to the absolute demoniacal power that could be unleashed in unmitigated fury upon the daughters and sons of God. Listen to John Hersey, an eyewitness to the tragedy of Hiroshima, and try to experience in your minds what he witnessed in actuality. "There were about twenty men ..... all in exactly the same nightmarish state; their faces were wholly burned, their eye sockets were hollow, the fluid from their melted eyes had run down their cheeks ..... their mouths were mere swollen, puss covered wounds, which they could not bear to stretch enough to admit the spout of a teapot ... ".

Dr. Elie Weisel, a Jewish poet and philosopher, who as a teenager knew exactly from first hand experience what holocaust is all about, even sees Auschwitz as a prelude to planetary holocaust, and has a right to ask us to listen when he says, "Never say that society will not do this or that; it will. Never seek shelter in convenient illusions that history will know when to stop so as not to destroy itself; it will not. This is a lesson I have learned years and massacres ago. Though uniquely Jewish, the holocaust has universal implications. What was done to one people affected mankind's destiny. Once unleashed, evil will recognize no boundaries. Auschwitz may belong to the past, but Hiroshima is part of our future ... Is there any doubt that proliferation will inexorably lead to nuclear destruction? One must be blind or suicidal not to see the signs. Once upon a time we believed in absolute truth; now we are cursed by the possession of absolute weapons."

When people say to me as a peace worker, "Don't forget 1939", and they mean don't forget how ill prepared we were to wage war, I say I will not forget 1939 but I will remember it in another context. I will remember it in the context of the time when Hitler was building up his diabolical war machine and when the churches largely remained silent. True, when he was engaging in his pogrom of the Jews, there were voices in the church raised in protest, but they were too few, too muted and too late. So while the nations prepare for what reputable scientists, both east and west, claim will be the end of life as we know it on the planet Earth — if the powers unleash the fury or even a fraction of that which they now have at their disposal — I, as a church leader, am not going to remain silent so that survivors, if there are any, and that in itself is a doubtful proposition, will be able to say, "Why did you, as a church leader, remain silent while the diabolical powers prepared for the holocaust of countless millions?" If any two individuals were standing in your town, one at one end of the main street and one at the other, and were threatening each other in the manner that is now being done by the Pentagon and the Kremlin, and in their threats were likely to take down with them the whole populace of the town, they would be committed to an institution for dangerous psychopaths. So it is that Jonathan Schell in a subsequent article to his book, "Fate of the Earth ...." writes, "The challenge is to unmake the choice of reasoning that locks our inaction, to break through the shield of political impossibility and to chart the path that leads back to survival."

The range of voices supporting the contention that something must be done and done speedily if we are not to reach this sorry end is both eloquent and far-reaching. Let me quote some of them. Billy Graham said, "The present insanity of the global arms race, if continued, will lead inevitably to a conflagration so great that Auschwitz will seem like a minor rehearsal." Two hundred and thirty-eight bishops of the Roman Catholic Church in the United States of America addressing fifty-one million members said, "Roman Catholics in military service should refuse an order to detonate a nuclear weapon — even if the order comes from the President of the United States." This resolution was based in part on the findings of the Nurenburg trials "that soldiers are obliged to refuse to obey immoral orders." The United Church General Council stated "because we are in covenant with the God of truth; we will not believe the claims of governments or military powers which hold sway by fear and seduce the people of the nations to expend their resources on arms and not on bread ..... because we are people of the Cross and acquainted with grief, we will reject and name the false gods of national security, national or racial superiority, economies based on the production of arms, and a false peace which depends on terror and not on justice." Robert MacNamara, former Secretary of Defence in the American government, referred to the present build-up in weaponry in his own country as a form of "insanity" and in this he included SDI or "Star Wars". The medical profession refers to the possibility of nuclear war as "the final epidemic." The minority report contained in the inter-party Parliamentary Committee report of our own government concluded with these words .... "The people not immediately burned to death (in a nuclear war) will be blown apart or asphyxiated or would find themselves in a nightmare world populated by the dead, the dying and the insane." I put it this way myself, "To push the button that would unleash a nuclear holocaust would be to break the first commandment and indeed, it might be the equivalent of committing the unforgivable sin." In other words, if there were some kind of winners emerged from such a conflict, they would be like General Sylvanus in the epic Massada, who, after conquering the mountain and seeing nothing around him but death and devastation, said, "We've won a rock, in the midst of a wasteland, on the shores of a poison sea."

We know this. We all know it. Statesmen know it, evangelists, theologians, medical scientists, nuclear physicists, generals, rear admirals, politicians ..... they all know it. Then how is it we can sit back and generate more passion about the Blue Jays, the Calgary Flames or the Saskatchewan Rough Riders than we can about the issue of peace?

Part of the reason surely is that we are afraid to face up to the reality of the situation. We fall back on worn out cliches such as, "If you want peace prepare for war." "Better dead than Red." "You can't trust the Russians." The worst of all of these glib responses is the one with theological implications that suggest God has planned it this way and that the open conflict between the East and the West is in accordance with God's holy will, that it would usher in the millenium and bring those who are the elect to their desired haven. Nothing could be more pronounced in flirting with blasphemy than that, and yet it is a position espoused by no less than President Ronald Reagan himself. Let me produce the evidence for such a statement. In an interview with Jim Bakker in 1980, Mr. Reagan said, "We may be the generation that sees Armageddon." In a report by Rev. Jerry Falwell in 1981, the President is quoted, "Jerry, I sometimes believe we are heading very fast for Armageddon right now." In a conversation with the American Israel Public Affairs Committee in 1983, Reagan said, "You know, I turn back to your ancient prophets in the Old Testament and the signs for telling Armageddon, and I find myself wondering if — if we are the generation that's going to see that come about." And in an interview in People Magazine, in December of that same year he said, "There have been times in the past when people felt the end of the world was coming, and so forth, but never anything like this." And finally this above all, "Libya has now gone Communist, and that's a sign that the day of Armageddon isn't far off .... everything is falling into place, it can't be long now ..." It is small wonder that Gary Lautens, editor emeritus of the Toronto Star, in an incisive article on this subject referred to Ronald Reagan as "the most dangerous man in the world."

Happily there are some antidotes to offset these perverted theological notions. One of them came to me, not from a theologian, or even a student of the Bible, but from a former captain of a nuclear submarine who worked for the Pentagon and is now a member of the Peace Research Institute. I sat beside Captain James Bush, to whom I am now referring, on the steps of Parliament Hill at a recent Hiroshima Day observance. Here is a man still in his fifties who had reached the pinnacle of his career and who occupied a secure and prestigious position in the American military. He gave all of this up to become a peace worker and spends his time shuttling back and forth across the continent speaking and working for peace. I asked him what brought him to this conclusion. (I know that "metanoia", that is "an about turn" is both a mental and moral possibility. But I am always interested in the motivation for it.) Captain Bush told me that he was in charge of one of the most powerful of American nuclear submarines in the Mediterranean theatre of operations. "I knew everything there was to know about the craft on which I was the Commanding Officer," he said. "For fifteen years," he continued, "I was in charge of a nuclear submarine which had at its command a hundred times the fire power of the bomb that was dropped on Hiroshima." There was, however, one thing they had not taught Jim Bush, and it was the one thing he could not handle. "They did not teach me," he told his Ottawa audience, "how to handle it if I got an order to fire all the power there was at my disposal ... And if I was the first person to receive such an order I would also be the first person in history to have killed in one moment of time more people than any other human being who has ever lived." This is what they did not teach the nuclear submarine captain, and, of course, it cannot be taught to any rational human being.

It is people like Captain Jim Bush, Rear Admiral Eugene Caroll and our own Canadian General George Johnston, as well as Giff Gifford of "Veterans for the prevention of nuclear war" who stand out as powerful allies of those who work for peace from a different bench mark. It is the passion of these people that I find most inspiring. When Elie Weisel, whom I quoted before, is pictured on the television screen addressing the President of the United States before his visit to West Germany where it was the President's intention to visit the cemetary where SS troops are buried, but *not* to go to one of the memorial concentration camps, Weisel said, "Mr. President, if I were to begin to name the children whom I have seen thrown into the fiery furnace, it would take me from now until the time I would die to repeat all their names, and even then I would not have accomplished the task. It is to these places, Mr. President, you should be going and bearing witness against this kind of infamy." That is why I maintain that since the Nuremburg trials have indicated that it is a crime against humanity to build concentration camps and the fiery furnaces into which the children were thrown, then it must also be a crime against humanity to build fiery furnaces which will be thrown *on* the children. There is no difference morally, ethically or theologically between throwing the child in the furnace and throwing the furnace on the child. To prepare the material and the process for either of these deeds must be something aginst which the Lord God Jehovah cries out with all the combined passion of the prophets of Israel and of the New Testament. I simply want to join my feeble voice with theirs.

But we are not people without hope. And I want to make two references to that in conclusion. When I joined the million people who walked for peace prior to the second United Nations session on disarmament in New York, I found myself walking side by side with a young American couple, as we went down First Avenue from Daghammersjold Blvd. toward Forty Second Street, where we were to turn down to Central Park where the rally was being held. The young couple asked where I was from and when I told them Canada, the woman said to the man, "Why don't you ask this Canadian the question you have been asking me?" He replied that he was simply asking the question, "Why am I out here? There are a dozen things I could be doing today besides being on this walk, and I wonder why I am here?" I knew that I had to leave the walk at Thirty-eighth Street to come back to Toronto to keep a speaking engagement so only had a few minutes to talk with them. "I don't know why you are out here," I responded. "All I can do is tell you why I am here. I am here mainly because of two groups of people we saw go by in this peace walk. They were the survivors of Hiroshima, the old men being led along by the grandchild because they were blind, the old women being pushed in wheelchairs alongside those who were on crutches; yet none of them so very old except for what had happened to them at Hiroshima. And there were their friends who were too weak to walk but were sitting in chairs by the curbside watching their friends go by." ... "Then after them," I continued, "there came the children. They had their balloons, their skipping ropes, their songs and their dances and their cheery smiles and their sheer enjoyment of a parade. I do not want to see those children have to go through what the survivors of Hiroshima went through, that is why I am here." "Well," he replied, "that helps a bit. But only a bit. I still feel like a grain of sand on the seashore." I looked up and saw the sign marking Thirty-eighth Street and knew I had to leave him in less than ten seconds, so I simply reached out my hand, shook hands with both of them, wished them God's speed and said, "Sir, you may feel like a grain of sand on the seashore. But don't forget it is the totality of the grains of sand on the seashore that holds back the tide."

I tell you that because I want every person who reads these words to know that it is as the Proverb says, "The water that wears the stones". It is the individual who decides in the contest of good and evil, of truth and justice, where the stubborn ounces of his'her moral weight will repose. There may be times when in doing so you feel like the grain of sand, but don't forget it is all the grains of sand together that hold back the tide.

Hope through people committed to the Shalom Kingdom
In spite of all this we are not as those who have no hope. Nor is this hope based on a facile optimism. It is hope that comes through the fact that people in different parts of the world share a common hope through common faith. Some of us are more free to express it than others.

A few years ago I made my second visit to the Soviet Union. A peace mission from a Toronto based peace group was sent to Moscow[1] and another to Washington. We each had the same message. It consisted of two thousand letters collected from Children in Canada and addressed to the children of the USA and the USSR; as well there was a one-page statement addressed to Mr. Reagan and Mr. Andropov which said in effect: "In the name of God stop this insane build-up of these arsenals of mega death proportions."

When we were in Moscow on Thursday evening we attended the Evangelical Baptist Church in the heart of the city. The church seats one thousand people and was packed with people in corridors and adjacent rooms. The minister said it would be filled again Friday and Saturday evening and for two services on Sunday.

The service lasted two hours and although offered in Russian, was obviously very evangelical in nature. Two hymns were, "What a Friend We Have in Jesus" and "I am Thine O Lord, I have heard Thy Voice." Clifford Elliott and I each spoke

---

1 The Moscow group consisted of: Rev. Clifford Elliott; Sr. Mary Jo Leddy; Fr. Paul Hansen; Ms. Dedrie McLaughlan; Rev. John Hess and Rev. Clarke MacDonald.

briefly, through an interpreter, about our peace mission. We based what we had to say on the Gospel. At the conclusion of the service they sang for us in Russian and English the words of: "God be with you 'till we meet again." Following this we all went out the central isle of the church together. People were reaching out to us from two, four and five deep from the end of the seat. They grasped our hands, some embraced us in tears and kept repeating over and over — "Mira!" -"Mira!" I turned to the minister and asked: "What does this word "Mira" mean?" "That means," he replied: "Shalom" or "Peace". They are asking you to take our Shalom to the people of Canada. Greet them for us with the sign of 'Peace' ". I do that now, from the people of the USSR to the people of Canada — 'Shalom' — 'Peace', in the name of Christ. I also thought of the words of General Dwight Eisenhower, a former president of the United States: "I believe people want peace so much that politicians and militarists had better get out of their way and let them have it."

So we are not as those who have no hope. Our hope is not just in people but in people who heed the word of Scripture: "Therefore seek peace and pursue it."

Thanks be to God. Amen.

THE VOICE OF THE UNKNOWN SOLDIER
Bright Shiny Bomb
by
Clarke McDonald

(Reflections on the increase in weapons of mass-destruction)

> Bright shiny bomb,
> How we should trust you!
> Protector of the human race
> Our Deliverer
> Standing there — ever alert,
> Nose cone pointing forward and ready —
> Ready to do the bidding
> Or Pentagon or Kremlin;
> To defend the one against the other.
> The first to overkill the second
> Twenty-five times;
> The second to overkill the first
> Seventeen times.

> When it happens
> The earth will tremble,
> The foundation quiver,
> Carogenic rain will fall,
> Upon the woman with child
> The child with the woman,
> The man in field or factory.
> The rivers will die,
> The fields will no longer bring forth fatness;
> From the mountains and hills we will hear

Neither song of bird or foot-fall or deer.
All we will hear is
The cry — the cry —
From parched throats,
"Bright shiny Bomb —
Why did we ever trust you?"

(These lines were written in the sixties when-even some churches were putting their trust in MAD (Mutual Assurred Deterrence). Fortunately this idoltry has diminished and the churches call the build-up of megadeath weapons by it's right name — Insanity.)

THE VOICE OF THE
UNKNOWN SOLDIER[1]

Text: "If the Lord does not protect the city (read 'nation', 'planet') it does no good for the sentries to stand guard."

Psalm 127:1.

I choose this text because on November 11th we observe what in Canada is known as 'Remembrance Day'.

On this morning, at eleven o'clock, in villages, hamlets, towns and cities all across this land, people will pause to remember. Some will only remember what they have read or heard since they have no personal experience of 1914-18 or 1939-45 or of other wars. I may be one of the least militaristic minded among the persons gathered here today. Yet, I have no hesitation in wearing the poppy in remembrance and the dove of peace — the symbol of a peace worker. For me the most tender moment in our national life is eleven o'clock on Remembrance Day when the White Cross mother lays a wreath at the cenotaph in Ottawa in memory of her children and others who died in war.

WHAT WILL WE REMEMBER?

As for me I will remember a day in May, 1945. The sun was shining and the farm of Mr. and Mrs. Lewis Murray, nes-

1. This sermon was broadcast from Thornhill United Church, Ontario, on the C.B.C. *Meeting Place,* November 9, 1986.

tled in the highlands of Cape Breton, was a scene of harmony and beauty as I approached it walking up the long, steep laneway. But I was about to bring a discordant note into that personal scene. I had to tell them that their son Jamie — as fine a lad as ever donned a Canadian uniform — had been killed in action. They had known for some weeks that the war was about to end and were looking forward with eager anticipation to Jamie's return, when he would take over the farm from the faltering hands of his father.

I will remember Roy. He sat next to me in Grade 12 in New Glasgow High School, Nova Scotia. He was an absolute whiz in mathematics, because I was such a dud in this subject, I valued his presence. You won't find his name recorded in the book of Remembrance in the Peace Tower in Ottawa. He went to England on his own when the war broke out and before the R.C.A.F. was established. He joined the R.A.F. and was one of the first Canadian casualities.

I will remember Cliff. For ten years we attended a one-room school together. Boys used to vie with each other to get Cliff on their side in a ball game because he could run like a deer. When he came back from the war he didn't run any more. He spent the rest of his days pushing a wheelchair up and down the corridors of Camp Hill Hospital.

OTHER PEOPLE, OTHER MEMORIES

People will have their own memories. Some will remember a lad who went off with a cheery, "I'll be seeing you when I get back," but they know he could have omitted the "when I get back" part. Others will remember the camaraderie of the mess hall or the barracks; or the lonely hours in a dugout; the frustrating ones on the drill square parade ground with some arrogant drill sergeant, the long hours in some torpedo infested waters; the bursting of shells; the whine of engines. Some will remember mud and blood in the darkness, spades in the darkness, curses and death in the darkness. Some will recall the times when they "slipped the surly bonds of earth and danced the skies on laughter silvered wings." But whatever crosses the screen of memory, we know that we will remember.

NOT TO REMEMBER — AN ACT OF BETRAYAL

We will remember because we know not to do so would be an act of betrayal. The first time I visited Westminster Abbey in London, England, the place that attracted me most was not the tombs, plaques and statues erected to the memory of kings, queens and princesses, some of whom were little more than part of a royal mafia. The place where I spent most time was right inside the massive Abbey doors in the well-cared-for area where the body of the unknown soldier reposes. This soldier, unknown as to name or number, unknown as to place of birth or family, as to race or creed — was known only for this — he gave his all. It is the only burial place in the floor of the Abbey that is protected from the footsteps of worshippers or sightseers. On it are the words commemorati ng the time when the leaders and the people, kings, princesses and commoners of the land, joined in tribute as the remains of the "unknown soldier", brought back from the battlefield, were committed to their final resting place. Being right in front of the doors means that kings and queens in procession to their coronations, weddings, or the funerals of their peers have to walk around it. But that is good because it compels them to remember.

STANDING BY THE TOMB

As I stood by the tomb, and later as I reflected on the experience, I imagined that I heard the firm steady voice of the unknown soldier echoing in the forest of pillars, sounding above the music from the throat of the mighty organ, and causing the interminable chatter of tourists to fade away. He said something like this:

"I came at the call of my country. But don't make too much of that. It was not pure patriotism that took me in. I had no job at the time. I was a statistic so far as my country was concerned.

Many times I stood in a breadline at a church mission or slept on a park bench during the depression. Some people called me a bum, others said I was a hobo. But then when they gave me a uniform, a rifle, a day's pay and three square meals, this hobo became a hero overnight. So don't make a saint of me. But don't make a devil of me either. As a matter of fact I might be quite at home with some of the chaps you call saints in the Bible. I was a struggling sinner like the rest of you. As a youngster I never stopped to think much about God. But then I discovered I needed God and I found him. As someone put it, 'there are no atheists in fox holes.' It was hell for us sometimes. I remember the night my chum got his eyes blasted out and I had to help him back from the front line. I knew he would never see again but I kept telling him, 'it will be alright, it will be alright''. Or when Joe private lost his legs and I carried him back of the lines and when Corporal Tommy died in my arms and asked me to say a prayer — I wasn't sure what to say. Then I remembered 'the Lord is my shepherd' and 'our Father who art in Heaven'. I didn't think it was much of a prayer but Tommy thanked me. It must have helped him. I used to lie in my bunk and think about my mother. She talked about God being near all the time, how He guided her and helped her in life. She was always pestering me to go to church with her. If I could go back now, probably I would. But then it would depend on whether or not what is happening there is real. You see I can't take anything that's phony anymore."

So we will remember because not to do so would be an act of betrayal.

TO REMEMBER IS TO LEARN

We will remember because of the lessons we can learn. Again, the unknown soldier speaks as I listen in a mood of reverie:

"I've got something special to say to the church. You see I fought what I was told would be a war to end wars — that was in 1917. Then they tell me that my son fought a war in 1939 'to make the world safe for democracy.' And they say there have been over a hundred smaller wars since that time, and democracy is in a more precarious position in the world now than it has been for decades. So somebody isn't doing a very good job. I am not blaming the preachers and the church for everything, but they do have a responsibility. I heard one of our generals say to a group of padres one day, 'it's your business to make my business impossible.'

I remember things people used to say in the church and about religion when I was back home and I liked what I heard. I recall one minister we had who talked a lot about putting your faith to work. He talked about things like 'Christianity in overalls'. I lived in a coal mining town and he talked about 'if Jesus were a coal miner'. Some people didn't like it because he preached that at a time when miners were trying to form a labor union. He talked about people being of equal worth and was angry at the way a black family was treated in our community. He tried to get Protestants and Roman Catholics working together. Some folks said, 'it's alright as long as he doesn't carry it too far.' Others said he wasn't 'spiritual enough', and that you shouldn't talk about politics and things like that from the pulpit.

But you know out there in the trenches it didn't seem to matter if a fellow is Black or White or Roman Catholic or Protestant or what he is. And after all it was the politicians who declared war, wasn't it? We were talking about this in the barracks one night and there was this fellow who knew his Bible well. I came to the conclusion after the discussion that Jesus was OK, but somewhere we have missed something he was trying to tell us. I'm not sure what we missed but I hope you people in the church will discover it and apply it. So tell the preachers for me that they have got to stop pussyfooting around and preach more real Jesus religion. A way of life that has the tough fibre of real love in it. Because that's the only thing that will stop war. Tell the politicians they have got to stop the double talk — extolling freedom and then going out to buy up votes. They've got to put ethical principles ahead of political expediency. Tell the big shots in the world of finance and business that their money won't get them to Heaven. God was nearer to me in a foxhole than He was at a cocktail party on Golden Avenue. So while you folks are busy, remember, just remember — you have got to trust God, live straight and love your neighbour, or we are headed for another war as sure as fate.''

FROM THE ABBEY TO EDINBURGH CASTLE

And so I left my imagining and remembering with the unknown soldier. A few days later I was standing beside a woman I had never met in the museum section of Edinburgh Castle in Scotland. We were looking at the metal balls and chains with which soldiers used to do battle in person to person combat. Admittedly they were hideous-looking instruments. She said: "My, weren't people cruel back in those days. I'm glad we don't do those things to people any more." "No", I replied, "We've learned a lot since then. Now somebody can press a button and barbecue a whole city in a matter of minutes."

LOOKING AT THE CAUSES OF WAR

Another reason why we must remember is because not to remember is to repeat the mistakes of history. One of those mistakes is to offer simplistic answers to the complex causes for war. It was Kaiser William, Emperor Hirohito, Adolph Hitler, Joe Stalin and people like that who caused war. But we know it is not that simple. Dr. George Wilson of Dalhousie University used to distinguish between "causes" for war and "occasions" for war. An occasion for war might be the Kaiser violating a treaty with Belgium, or Hitler invading Poland, or the Japanese bombing Pearl Harbour. But the causes of war are different.

Listen a moment to Saint James. "What causes wars, and what causes fightings among you? Is it not your passions that are at war in your members? You desire and do not have; so you kill. And you covet and cannot obtain; so you fight and wage war." Messrs. Reagan and Gorbachov should have had these words in capital letters on the wall of their meeting room in Iceland lately. We do not think of passions here as we think of them in terms of some of St. Paul's writings dealing with sexuality. The passions referred to here are the passions that drive the mafia; the passions that drove the American involvement in Vietnam, the Soviet involvement in Afganistan; that fuel the fires of conflict in the Middle East or Ireland; and that cause death and destruction in Latin America. In microcosm and in less violent form they are the same passions that drive corporations in their acquisitiveness, governments in their covetousness and religious groups in their arrogance. They are the same passions that drive churches when they are more concerned about institution s than they are about people ... more concerned to preserve doctrinal purity than they are to bear witness to the unity in Christ. Thus, with consummate insight, St. James views this as the root of our problem. Violent passion, acquisitiveness , pride and violence become a way of life when we forsake the rugged love revealed in Jesus Christ. None of us can completely wash our hands and escape responsibility in this matter.

I remember back in the thirties gathering up old pieces of scrap iron, broken harrow teeth, old cream separators and other bits and pieces of farm machinery. These were picked up by a local scrap merchant and I didn't know that tons and tons of it were shipped to Japan. So when the hero in "Chariots of Fire" died in a Japanese prison camp, he may have been beaten with the butt of a rifle made from the scrap iron of somebody's cream separator. Many people in this continent made a healthy profit by manufacturing for the war machine and helped build up both sides before the second world war.

REMEMBERING IN HOPE

But we are not people without hope. Our hope is steadfast and sure. One man I know saw it in a dark hour in the human story. It was August 6, 1945, when the atomic bomb was dropped on Hiroshima. Dr. Kenneth Boulding, a teacher, economist, poet and philosopher, hearing the news wrote words which he shared with me a few years ago.

"In all this world two kingdoms now remain,
The Kingdom of this world and of the Lord.
The one, content no longer with the sword
That takes but one life, now with murderous rain
Blankets whole towns with ruin, death and pain.
The other is not yet seen, not yet out poured
In visible might, yet here and there adored
By those whose hearts are bound in love's bright chain.

And you must choose — you are no longer free
To dally with them both — the time's too late.
Our cities all must suffer Sodom's fate,

And where's the ark to ride a brimstone sea,
If not a manger — what, if not the blood
of Christ, can quench the fire of this last flood?"

Thanks be to God. Amen.

PRAYER —
A PERSONAL APPROACH

"The best relation to our spiritual home is to be near enough to love it.

But the next best is to be far enough away not to hate it."

G.K. Chesterton

Dr. John Baillie opened the Gifford Lectures in 1961 by telling of a student who sat staring at an examination paper but wrote nothing down:

"What ails you?" asked the examiner:
"I don't know the answers," replied the student.
"Then," said the examiner: "Put down what you know."

When it comes to prayer, its power, its grace and the way some people try to manipulate God — I don't have all the answers but have simply "put down what I know."

PRAYER — A PERSONAL APPROACH

(Reprinted with permission from Touchstone)

Ever since human beings first realized the power of forces beyond themselves — be they sun, wind or lightning, they have prayed. As they associated these powers with various features of their common life — daylight and darkness; the changing seasons; the growing of crops; the ebb and flow of the tides; the strength of the mountains; the mystery of life and death — they tied their prayer life to objective and identifiable aspects of life around them. The sun, the moon, the volcano became the object of worship. For safety sake they did not confine themselves to just one of these gods but had a god for each occasion and when they ran out of gods selected from the natural scheme of things they created their own.

GOD IS GOD — GOD IS ONE

We Christians do not realize, sometimes, how much we owe to the revolutionary insight of our Hebrew ancestors when with consumate audacity they dared to announce — "The Lord our God - the Lord is One." That shook the whole theological framework of the time and succeeding generations to its very foundation. It also made possible God's own revelation of Self through the Person of Jesus Christ. Dr. T.S. Blank, a Hebrew scholar from Cincinnati, speaking in Holy Blossom Temple in Toronto, told of a student who put this enigmatic line in one of his essays. "The problem with monotheism," he wrote, "is that it is not fair to the other gods!" Indeed it isn't and it never intended to be. It was out to destroy the notion of other gods

126

not to be fair to them. After all, why do you need to be fair to that which does not exist?

Our prayers are directed to the Lord God Jehovah revealed to us in Jesus Christ. It is important to say that at the beginning. We, as Christians, do not pray to a capricious monster lurking in the shadows or to a malevolent force residing in the tombs. We pray to God who is — whose only designation is "I am" and whose face we have seen in Jesus of Galilee and Calvary.

"THROUGH JESUS CHRIST OUR LORD"

This means that if our prayers are to be true to that benchmark they need to be offered in the "Name" of, in the Spirit of, that same Christ. When I pray then I need to pray in a manner that reflects the mind of Christ. That is the meaning of praying "through Jesus Christ Our Lord." It is as if to say: "God if this prayer cannot go through Christ, get the approval of Christ and be sanctioned by Christ, then God — for Christ's sake — ignore it."

THE HOLY SPIRITS' PRESENCE

Our assurance of the nearness of God to whom we pray is confirmed by the knowledge of the nature of God revealed in Jesus Christ. It follows then that our conviction God does hear our prayers varies in almost direct proportion to our faith (our faith not merely our intellectual assent or belief) in the Holy Spirit. The Biblical underpinning for that statement is not far to seek. "Deep calleth unto deep." Jesus was "in the Spirit" when he went into the wilderness; when he prayed in Gethsemane and on Calvary. St. Paul trusted the Spirit to aid with his prayers. "The Spirit makes intercession for us." The well known and lesser known saints since that time have likewise sensed the Spirit like "the hound of heaven" — persuing them "down the nights and down the days, down the arches of the years..." and we still flee from the spirit for the same reason, "lest having (Christ) I should have nought beside."

The experience of the two men on the road to Emmaus confirms that to pray, as if God were present because we believe God is present, is to set the heart aglow, clarify the meaning of scripture and give us winged feet to carry the good news back to Jerusalem — or to the ends of the earth. To pray without any sense of the Presence of God is a bland and sterile experience — but is nevertheless no good reason to give up praying because God has a way of breaking through even then.

THE DIFFERENCE CHRIST MAKES IN PRAYING

Here is the difference God/Christ present in the Holy Spirit's Presence makes in one's prayer life. Back in the 1940's a young man went from Canada to India.[1] He saw the poverty, the disease ridden bodies, the starving and dying children on the streets of Calcutta. He threw up his hands and cried in desperation: "My God why do you allow this?" He concluded that if God was almighty and did nothing about this then love was lacking, if, on the other hand God was loving and did nothing about it this must be because God was impotent to effect any change. He came back to Canada and remained a skeptic and sometimes disillusioned man, albeit a very human individual, the rest of his days. About this same time a young woman went out to India from Albania.[2] She saw the same poverty, the same disease and suffering. She did not cry out "My God why?" but "My God what?" "What is your will for me in this?" "What do I need to do about it?" "What do I need to say to others to get them to help?" In essence she prayed. "God use me to bring relief to the suffering; food to the hungry and hope to the dying." That is the difference Christ makes in our approach to life and to prayer.

PRAYER AS A WAY OF LIFE

Prayer for me is more a way of life than it is an act of worship. I think this is what St. Paul meant when he said: "Pray without ceasing." He certainly did not mean to spend all your time on your knees — or all your time looking heavenward. "Why do you stand gazing up to heaven?" the risen Christ asked the bewildered disciples. Jesus warning about people who "in the market place make long prayers to be seen

1 The late Gordon Sinclair as reported by him on a number of occasions.
2 Mother Theresa.

128

of others"; could probably be rendered today — "Woe to those who on television make long prayers, but who when I was in prison, or hungry, or a stranger did not visit, feed or make me feel I was a person." Prayer as a way of life commits each day and each deed to God knowing that though the day will be blemished and the deeds will be imperfect, God whose "grace is heaped upon grace" will forgive and restore.

A PROCESS FOR PRAYING

One of the devotional hymns of the last generation had a line which went: "I ask no dream, no prophet ecstasies, no sudden rending of the veil of clay... but take the dimness of my soul away." It is this "dimness of the soul" that makes us so spasmodic and ineffective in prayer. Since so much of our religious and church life is tied to the notion of "process" let me suggest a process for prayer.

1. **Centre the mind upon God** — however you think of God. Begin where you are. Don't worry if someone else might think your approach primitive. God will begin with you as you are — you have to begin with God as you perceive God to be.

2. **Deepen your understanding of God** by reference to the Bible and other resources. Get to know the passages that speak to you about God and refer to them often before or during prayer. Skip, at least for the time being, the ones that seem foreign or speak less to you about God than you are able to see in Jesus Christ.

3. **Concentrate on the positive.** Think about — write down if need be — the things for which you have reason to give thanks. Bishop Tutu, who has more reason to complain than most of us, used the words: "Thank you God, thank you" — some forty times when he preached and prayed in a Toronto Church last year.

4. When you pray for others **picture the "Spirit of God"** — "the Living Spirit of Christ" — "the Holy Spirit" hovering over, around, beneath, above, within the one(s) for whom you are praying. I picture it like

I used to see the early morning mist hovering over the fields on my father's farm with the shafts of morning sunlight piercing through in light and warmth. Don't tell God what to do — just ask God to be there and to do what the God we've seen in Christ knows to be best. Trust God. God may not answer your words. God will answer your prayers.

A PERSONAL TESTIMONY

When my wife, a child, another loved one or someone for whom my prayers were asked and promised is being prayed for, this is the "process" I use. I never pray for things, I pray for people and the things necessary will be forthcoming — if we and they are open to God. When I was seriously ill in hospital on a couple of occasions I never prayed explicitly to be made better. I did pray for the strength to be and do what God wanted of me. This was on the basis of the promise: "As thy days so shall thy strength be." When two of our babies were very ill and later died Muriel and I did not demand of God that they be made well. We asked "if it be possible" may they be spared — if not may we be able to use this time to the glory of God. That is probably why when I visited a young mother in the hospital fifteen years later who had lost her baby she said: "Mr. MacDonald it is good of you to come but would you please ask Muriel to come to see me — you see — she's been where I am."

5. **Leave the outcome to God.** If we are not prepared to do this prayer may futile, frustrating and soul destroying. But to pray in this way makes it an exciting, meaningful act. We have either to acknowledge that God is God or put ourselves or something or someone else in God's place. This is a hazardous pursuit. It is also a seductive one. You can make a God of anything from money, to sex, to bombs or to the Bible. This is when we need to remember the revolutionary insight of our Hebrew ancestors in the faith: "The Lord our God is One ... you shall have no other gods before me."

PRAYERS AND POLITICS

"I cannot praise", said John Milton, "a cloistered and sequestered virtue that is afraid to sally forth." I cannot commend a prayer life that is all me and no one else.

"God bless me and my wife,
Our son John and his wife,
Us four,
And no more!"

The broken bruised ones of the world need our prayers. The power brokers of the world, the Reagans, Gorbachevs, Khomeinis, Qaddafis, Thatchers and Mulroneys need our prayers. So too do the little people who are favorably or adversely affected by what these people say and do. I am convinced that if the professing Christians around the planet would unite in prayer for peace and justice and back up their prayers by political action, we would see "a new heaven and a new earth" — not in the terms that John the Divine saw it but in the terms that Jesus meant when he taught us to pray:

"Thy kingdom come,
Thy will be done,
On earth as it is in heaven."

Even so, Lord Jesus — "Teach us to pray."

"Lord grant me the serenity to accept the things I
cannot change.
the courage to change the things I can
and the wisdom to know the difference." Amen.

This prayer was prepared one Sunday morning when I awoke to the beautiful scene of new fallen snow. It was part of a broadcast service from Saint Luke's Church, Toronto, that morning. Some said they found it to be a "healing prayer". It is shared now in relation to the message on the subject of prayer.

Almighty God — God of the seasons, we thank you for new fallen snow. Teach us today the lessons to be learned from this portion of your creative power. While the flakes all look the same yet each is different — so too while we speak of "the mass of humanity" or the "human race" — yet help us not to forget that everyone is a child before you — and help us, knowing our identity, to say "Lord what do you want me to do?"

Lord, teach us the lessons from new fallen snow.

As the snow is white and beautiful until it is touched by smoke and pollution, so our lives made in your image to show forth your glory are touched by sin and polluted by pride. We try to make them over after our own wills. As we make footpaths in the snow and someone else follows our markings, so help us to remember that in life we, by what we are and what we do, make a trail that others may follow to honor or dishonor — to life or to death.

Lord, teach us the lessons from new fallen snow.

The snow is driven by the will of the wind. It does not stay when the power of God would move it. So help us to be driven by the breath of your Spirit. Let us not stay when your power bids us to move — let us not be moved when the quiet hush of your Spirit bids us to remain. Help us to go and to come at your bidding.

Lord, teach us the lessons from new fallen snow.

The snow makes the world bright, we see our way easier in the dark when it is here. So may we shine as lights in this dark world, may people see their way better because our lives — like the snow makes the world brighter. As the world is brighter still when the snow reflects the glory of sun or moon — so may our lives reflect your glory and not try to shine in their own strength.

Lord, teach us the lessons from new fallen snow.

But the snow has to go. It has to be trod upon — it even has to be lost that it may be spared and receive a new garment of whiteness. The world touches it, the sun shines upon it. It feeds the rivers, the lakes and the seas. The vegetation of next harvest is watered by its sacrifice. Commerce and industry are aided by it. So may we be spent — poured out if need be — so may our lives be used. Help us not to be afraid to get our lily white garments of spirituality touched by the world. Out there where passions burn and life is hard on so many may we offer ourselves in sacrifice.

Lord, teach us the lessons from new fallen snow.

Yet the snow is driven back again to the bosom of the sky, so may we be drawn to you O God — drawn by the cords of love — at last even to the portals of Eternal Life there to meet God the Father — Christ our Brother and Holy Spirit — Mother of our Spirit.

Through Jesus Christ our Lord. Amen.

POSTLUDE
FAITH — LOVE AND PRAYER —
THESE THREE

[An address by Estella (Mrs. George D. MacDonald) at a
W.M.S. Rally — Pictou Presbyterial — 1959]
Following preparation of the manuscript for this book and upon
going through some papers I came across a copy of this address. It was a 'talk' my mother gave at a Women's Missionary
Society Rally in Pictou County in the mid-fifties. The manuscript was in her own handwriting. She had given it to me
sometime before her death in 1973 at the age of ninety-three.

I am amazed how relevant what she had to say then is to the
situation now. I am delighted also to see the affinity her thinking had with the tenor of what I have written. A quote from
her address captures my recollection of the sort of woman she
was: "Christ saw men and women not for what they were or
had done, but rather for what through the grace of God they
might become." A woman who heard my mother on this occasion said: "It is obvious that with two preacher sons, Peter
Stuart and Clarke, 'Mrs. George D' is the best preacher of the
three." I couldn't agree more! I am grateful to Bill Park who is
in charge of this project for his willingness to include this
postlude. CMD.

FAITH — LOVE AND PRAYER — THESE THREE

Test: "Put on the whole armour of God that ye may be able to withstand against the wiles of the devil."

Ephesians 6: 5-11

INTRODUCTION

Chief Justice Holmes of the United States was noted for his sound practical advice on any matter however great or however trivial, whether pertaining to his office as Chief Justice or pertaining to the problems of everyday life. One day he received a letter from a woman in which she said, "the church in our local community is fast falling into decay. We have tried every conveivable means to hold the church together. We have suppers and tea sales, we've had picnics and socials to no avail." What, she asked, would Justice Holmes suggest they do to keep the church alive. Justice Holmes replied in four simple words, "why not try religion?" We today are living in a world that has tried every conceivable means of existence. We don't have to enumerate them; we know them all as we turn the pages of history since the dawn of man. Down through the early days of civilization, the days of the prophets, the rise and fall of the great Roman Empire, the middle ages, the Reformation until today as we reach the half-way mark of the twentieth century, we stand on the threshold of the age of Atomic Energy. And just where do we stand today? How much nearer is mankind today to the ultimate goal of man than were those shepherds of Judea as they roamed the hills tending their flocks and on that first Christmas night heard the angel chorus sing, "Peace on earth, good will among men"?

We, today, are supposed to be living in a post-war era of peace and prosperity yet on every hand we see confusion and chaos, we see want and fear, pain and hunger stalking rampant through the world. We see godless communism pit itself against democracy, creed against creed, race against race, color against color, until we can almost hear the cry of humanity going to God and saying, "we've tried every conceivable means to hold the world together. We've had our suppers and our tea sales. We've had our picnics and our socials. What O God would you suggest that we do now?" And ringing down through the centuries comes this age old exhortation of Paul to the Ephesians, "Put ye on the whole armour of God."

AT THE CROSSROADS OF LIFE

Man has unloosed into the world today a power that, until a few years ago, was but a dream of a few scientists but that dream has now become a reality in the form of atomic energy. That energy if used aright can do much for the world but that energy if used amiss could well near obliterate humanity. Mankind is standing at the crossroads of life today as it has perhaps never stood before. On the one hand is oblivion, on the other the rugged trail that leads upward, ever upward toward the Kingdom of God, our Father in Heaven. At that crossroads stands Jesus saying today as he has never said before, "choose ye this day." If mankind is going to choose the way of Jesus Christ, then it has to start with people like ourselves. What then was the answer of Jesus? What was the source of Christ's great strength and fortitude that enabled him to meet the trials, troubles and temptations of life? He met them yet walked serenely through it all and in the end to triumph over death and the grave itself. There are many things that went into the making of the armour of Jesus Christ so let us consider for a few moments a few of the main parts and I think with these three the rest can be easily assembled in their proper places.

FAITH

The first of these is Faith. Faith is defined as being a belief or trust in some person or object to fulfil the purpose which it was intended to do. So when we profess our faith in Jesus Christ and his way of life we are saying we believe in a God who is able to guide us, guard us, strengthen us, and sustain us amid all that life may have in store for us. Yet how often we fail to show that faith as a working reality in our daily lives. We fail to feel the living presence of God — in fact we sometimes doubt if there is a God at work in the world at all. We all too often forget the blessings and joys which are ours and instead see only the hardship, the sorrows and disappointments. Dr. Nicholson, President of Pine Hill, was one of the delegates to the World Council of Churches which met in Amsterdam. When speaking of that Council he told of how it met in Amsterdam just when the tension between East and West was at its height in Berlin. The threat of a third great conflict hung like a pall of gloom over the meetings there. But he said the significant thing about it was that the delegates from Europe who knew the horrors, the hardships, the pain and suffering that war could bring, also knew from experience that in spite of all that war brings to them or takes from them, one thing it would not take away was their faith in a living Heavenly Father. With that conviction in their hearts they were ready to face the future with quiet confidence. That is the faith that Christ would have in all his followers for even in our darkest hour God is always at our side ready to help us if we but put our trust in him.

In that scene portrayed for us in the Bible where the disciples were out in a boat on the lake and a storm came up, they were in great danger of being shipwrecked. They saw a figure walking towards them on the water. At first they were frightened until they recognized it was the Master. Then Peter impetuous, impulsive Peter said, "Lord bid me to come to thee on the water." Jesus said "Come". Peter stepped over the side of the boat and began to walk towards Jesus, but when he saw the great waves rushing in on every side he became frightened and immediately he began to sink, and cried, "Lord save me or I perish". Jesus stretched out his hand, lifted him up saying,

"O thou of little faith. Wherefore didst thou doubt?" So when we become frightened and dismayed by the storm of life, if we but stop to listen, don't you think we too would hear Him saying, "O thou of little faith, wherefore didst thou doubt?"

LOVE

The second thing in the armour of Jesus was love. Christ's great love for his fellow man. The records of Jesus' life are full of evidence of his love for men, women and children. Time and again we read the words, "and Christ had compassion on them." Everywhere he went Jesus was known as the man who went about doing good, healing the sick, strengthening the weak, restoring sight to the blind, comforting the aged. Christ's love for his brother man was also revealed in that he called Matthew to be his disciple. Matthew was a despised and hated tax gatherer for the Roman oppression. He had stooped to the task of taking money from his fellow man and handing it over to the Roman authorities. He had even begun to hate himself but it seemed to him he had gone too far to change. But as Christ saw him sitting there at the seat of custom, he saw something else stir in Matthew's breast. Something so deep that Matthew himself perhaps was not aware of it and turning to him he said, "follow me". For Christ saw men and women not for what they were or had done but rather for what through the grace of God they might become. So it is in life. The happiest people are those who are always helping others and so forgetting their own wants and personal troubles. Those who see the best in neighbors and associates instead of the worst. So great was Christ's love for his fellow man that even in his hour of greatest pain and agony as he hung upon the Cross of Calvary he could look up into the heavens and say of those who had put him there, "Father forgive them for they know not what they do." So if we would have in our hearts the peace which God alone can give, then we too must have Christ's love and forgiving spirit toward our fellow men in our hearts.

PRAYER

Third in the armour of Jesus was prayer.

Christ spent many of His waking hours in prayer, in communion with His Father in Heaven, for prayer to Christ was a very important part of His everyday life. It was in prayer that Christ found His strength and faith renewed. After a busy day of teaching and healing He would seek out some quiet place where He would pray to God for guidance and help in the seemingly impossible task which lay before Him. Prayer is often a misunderstood and misinterpreted act of devotion. Many persons think of prayer as a means of getting what they want the easiest way possible. Then when their prayers go unanswered they fail to see any value or any good in prayer. But Christ never meant prayer to be anything like that. Christ said "whatsoever ye ask in my name I will do it." We all too often forget those three little words "in my name" and instead seek only our own personal desires taking no thought of God's great place in His universe. Then, above all, prayer is the submitting of our will to the will of our Heavenly Father. Christ exemplified this in his prayer in the garden of Gethsemane on the night in which he was betrayed. Christ was troubled that night as he climbed the Mount of Olives with his disciples. He knew what lay before Him on the morrow if he stayed at Jerusalem and how often the tempter must have spoken to him that night saying, "why not slip out through the East gate under cover of darkness and flee into the mountains, stay there until your enemies have left then come back and gather together your followers and start over again." Christ prayed fervently to his Father. "O God if it be possible grant that this cup shall pass from me." Then you note he came back and found his disciples asleep and he was annoyed. Waking them he said, "could ye not watch with me one hour?" He went back and prayed again and yet again. Then came the climax to that great prayer and it should be the climax of every prayer "nevertheless, not my will but thine be done." There Christ found the help that he needed. He went back and found his disciples asleep again and he said, "sleep on now and take your rest." He didn't then persevere any longer for he had found his help and his strength in submitting his will to the will of His Heavenly Father. So we have these three, Faith, Love and Prayer. If we take these and put them to work in our daily lives minute by minute and hour by hour then we will be ready to take our place in the Crusade for Christ and His Kingdom here in this Canada of ours and throughout the world. Then and only then will we truly understand and appreciate what the Hymn writer meant when he said "I know not what the future hath of marvel or surprise, assured alone that life and death, His mercy underlies."

Let us pray. O God, our Heavenly Father, help us to walk in thy ways and to live life in the calm assurance that thou art ever at hand to guide and strengthen us for we ask it in thy name. Amen.

DON'T STOP THE WORLD — WE HAVE A JOB TO DO

Suggestions for Reflection and/or Discussion.

1. Consider the decision of Captain James Bush to leave his nuclear sub and join the Peace Research Institute. What does this say about the "Catch-22" in which some people find their work places them?

2. "We are called to be obedient — we are not called to be popular."

   "We are called to be faithful — we are not called to be successful."

   Can you think of — and discuss local situations in which you and/or your congregation face this kind of choice.

3. What do the three letters from — the business man — the doctors — and the two women say about the pluralism of thought in our church?

4. What do they say about the variety of ideas in your group?

A FAITH FOR TOUGH TIMES

Suggestions for Reflection and/or Discussion.

1. Think about or discuss the statement by Eliel Weisel:

   "It is harder to believe in God than not to believe in God."

2. Do you think the response given about the Soviets being "very religious" because of devotion at Lenin's Tomb was justified?

3. "Name it and you can deify it. Some people make a god out of the Bible ... the Creed ... a Church ...a political party ..." etc. Discuss this statement and add alternative possible "gods" ...

BOTH SIDES NOW

Suggestions for Reflection and/or Discussion.

1. Discuss the meaning of a "full Gospel" in terms of the introduction to this sermon.

2. Study the Gospel of Saint Matthew 17: 1-21 in the light of the study included in this sermon — and beyond that.

3. What are the dangers and/or values in trying to "repeat" a spiritual experience?

4. From what "mountain tops" have you come to what "valleys" — how did you handle the tensions?

5. Discuss the "layman's witness" also in the light of the quote from

E. Stanley Jones.

THE CHRIST MIND IN MINISTRY FOR THE EIGHTIES

Suggestions for Reflection and/or Discussion

1. Do you think the theological underpinning (we don't mean simply quoting the Bible — but the broad sweep of theology written about in the Bible) is sufficiently evident in the preaching we hear today?

2. If not, what can all the people as "ministers" do to help rectify the situation?

3. What makes being a minister today more difficult than forty — or eighty years ago?

4. How can minister and people together enlarge their servant role?

5. Do you catch the "liberation" note in the Bible caught by "Cheryl" and "Rosa Parks"?

6. Discuss the episode "The Man in The Water". What do you learn from it?

THE CHURCH UNDER THE CROSS

Suggestions for Reflection and/or Discussion:

1. Discuss the contrast made in this sermon between the Bloor Street United Church Service and the electronic evangelist. How do we "trivialize the cross" in our experience today?

2. A United Church woman said recently: "If I were tortured I hope I would bear myself with dignity." Given the stark, sombre reports of Amnesty International do you think that is possible?

3. Discuss each of the three propositions:
   a) Choice b) Vulnerability c) The Cross as "grace heaped upon grace".

4. What does the story told by Eliel Wiesel tell us about the faith of our Jewish brother?

AMAZING GRACE

Suggestions for Reflection and/or Discussion

1. Discuss the statement:
   "The law as law cannot forgive. If it were to do so it would cease to be law. Only grace can forgive."

2. Consider Faith as a "gift" to be celebrated.

3. Discuss the understanding a Jew would have of the meaning of "law".

4. A number of people have found the "mitre box" story very meaningful. Read it aloud and discuss its meaning for you.

THE CHURCH AND POLITICS

Suggestions for Reflection and/or Discussion:

1. Discuss the opening statement about Church/State; God/ Good Government do you agree? If so, how do you apply it?

2. Is political neutrality possible — practical — (or advisable)?

3. Consider the "radicalism" of the prophets in the light of the definition — "getting to the root ....."

4. Professor R.B.Y. Scott made his statement about the "Relevance of the Prophets" almost four decades ago. Does it still fit in situations where your community has — or needs — a prophet?

5. Prayerfully consider the statement by the young woman in the GDDR — what does it say about our easy-going attitudes?

TELLING MY STORY
SHARING MY FAITH

Suggestions for Reflection and/or Discussion

1. Think of an early recollection of being a person that you are willing to share with others.

2. Does this recollection have any religious or spiritual overtones or implications?

3. How can we handle the "complexities" which we perceive to be part of life as adolescent understanding takes over?

4. Discuss the "break through" when reading Ephesians, Chapter 2, verse 8 does such an experience have any meaning for you?

5. How do you view the notion of what Donald Soper called a "second funnel" for ministry?

PROPHETS THEN AND PROPHETS NOW

Suggestions for Reflection and/or Discussion

1. Discuss prophet as "the one who announced the purpose and activity of God." As you do this you may want to look at Isaiah 58:1-10; Micah 6:6-8; Isaiah 2:1-4; Jeremiah 10:1-10; Hosea 14:4-8; Amos 5:14-24.

2. Discuss the "prophetic act" of Lydia Gruchy in pressing for ordination fifty years ago. Are women in the Roman Catholic Church today who press for ordination to the priesthood being prophetic?

3. Can you think of and talk about dealing with "aberrations of the prophetic role" today?

4. Can you name a prophet in your group — church — community? Does she/he fit the "marks of the prophet referred to in this sermon?

5. Discuss the adequacy or otherwise of the "vision" for the church with which this message concludes.

THE VOICE OF THE UNKNOWN SOLDIER

Suggestions for Reflection and/or Discussion:

1. Those who are old enough to remember may want to share thoughts about:
   (a) Where you were and how you felt in September 1939 when war was declared.
   (b) Where you were and how you felt in May 1945 when the war in Europe ended.
   (c) Where you were and how you felt on August 6, 1945, when the atomic bomb was dropped on Hiroshima (re-read Boulding's poem before doing so).

2. There is something phoney about phrases like:

   "a war to end war" ... "a war to make the world safe for democracy" Are there phoney phrases today — like — the MX missile is called "the peace keeper" — or consider phrases like "mutual assured deterrence."

3. Consider George Igantieff's words opposing nuclear weapons: "let's have no incineration without representation."

4. Study the words of St. James, Chapter 4 — "What causes wars and fightings among you ...?"